PHILOSOPHIES OF EDUCATION

'TO MY PARENTS'

Published by
S.B. Nangia
A.P.H. Publishing Corporation
4435–36/7, Ansari Road, Darya Ganj,
New Delhi-110002
Phone: 011–23274050
e-mail: aphbooks@gmail.com

2026

Rs. 1995/-

Typeset by
Ideal Publishing Solutions
C-90, J.D. Cambridge School,
West Vinod Nagar, Delhi-110092

Printed at
RD DIGITAL PRINTERS
Ansari road , Daryaganj, Delhi-110002

Philosophies of Education

A.S. SEETHARAMU

A P H PUBLISHING CORPORATION
4435-36/7, ANSARI ROAD, DARYA GANJ
NEW DELHI-110 002

PREFACE TO THE SECOND EDITION

This reference work intended for use by advanced students and teachers of the subject has been received well. This prompted the author and the publishers to revise and update it. The work of revision has been completed while only the chapter on Language Analysis has been updated to some extent. The author would like to acknowledge his thanks to Prof. Paul Hirst, Professor of Education, Cambridge University, himself a Philosopher and language analyst, for his valuable and critical comments on the earlier version of this chapter. A few educational philosophers who have influenced educational thinking or practice or both in India have been included in this edition.

It is hoped that the users will respond to this edition equally well as they done before. The author looks forward to critical reviews of the book addressed to him or to professional journals which will be useful for future revisions.

A.S. SEETHARAMU

Professor of Education
Institute for Social and Economic Change,
Bangalore-560072

PREFACE TO THE FIRST EDITION

I always felt that a teacher of Philosophy of Education should maintain a skeptical approach to the subject and present different points of view with utmost objectivity. He ought not to reflect his preferences in his teaching. He should encourage his students to reflect over the different points of view and in the process develop their own. Intellectual honesty, objectivity in judgment and fairplay in presentation should be the guiding ideals at higher levels of teaching. I have attempted this reference work with such a framework of mind. However, I do not claim total success in my attempt. I am aware that in certain subtle ways I am myself influenced by the existential outlook on life.

I thank Smt. Usha Ramkumar, Technical Assistant, ISEC, for preparing the bibliography.

I welcome, rather look foward, to criticism of the work.

A.S. SEETHARAMU

FOCUS OF THE WORK

The work consists of two parts. The first part covers a discussion of the meanings of philosophy and education and their mutual relation. There is also a discussion of the various issues in education in the light of the traditional schools of philosophy that have influenced educational thought, such a Naturalism, Idealism, Pragmatism and Realism. Later, a discussion of the contemporary schools of philosophy such as existentialism and language analysis and their implications to education follows.

The second part consists of a discussion of the concept and functions of aims in general. It also discusses a few aims of education of contemporary interest such as national integration, international understanding, democracy and the relative importance of individual and social aims in education.

In the end there is also a discussion of the place and importance of the curriculum and its organisation, short-comings of the present day curriculum and remedies to overcome them.

CONTENTS

CHAPTER 1

Meanings of Philosophy

It is rather difficult to define philosophy in a way that is universally acceptable. There are different meanings for philosophy. These meanings correspond to the diversities of life. As these meanings of philosophy are at variance with each other the meanings of education which depend upon the former also vary. The following meanings of philosophy have been useful for a systematic understanding of education.

Philosophy as Love of Knowledge

This is the etymological meaning of philosophy. The origin of the word is from two Greek words 'Philos' and 'Sophia'. 'Philos' means love and 'Sophia' means wisdom or knowledge. The ancient Greeks believed that a person becomes wise by knowledge and understanding. There is an observation by Plato in his 'Republic' which reflects the belief that philosophy is that love of knowledge which makes a man wise and to live wisely was the ideal of human life in those times : "He who has a taste for every sort of knowledge and who is curious to learn and is never satisfied may be justly termed a philosopher."[1] It is to be noted in the above definition that a philosopher is to be interested in 'all types' of knowledge. A physicist is interested in the physical processes of the universe, a biologist in the biological universe, a sociologist in the social life and likewise persons of different disciplines have their focus of interest. It is quite possible for them to limit their interest in such a way. But when it is said that to become a philosopher one must get interested in all these disciplines it may be wondered whether such multi-dimensional interest is possible at all. But a great score of philosophers of the world have provided an answer through their life and works. To illustrate, Aristotle who was one of the great philosophers of Greek culture was a repository of contemporary Knowledge. His works such as *De Anima* (meaning 'of the soul' and a book on psychology), *Politics* (a book useful to students of politics and education), *Poetics* (a book on literary criticism), *Ethics* and other works on science reflect his breadth of interest and depth of scholarship. A few centuries earlier, that is till recently, a number of disciplines which enjoy an independent status in the present universities were considered as a part of philosophy. Physics, Chemistry, etc. were called as Natural Philosophy ; Politics, Economics, Sociology, etc., were called as Moral Philosophy and Psychology was included under Mental Philosophy. Even now there has been no shift from the focus of interest in philosophy. Philosopher is interested in the first principles and final conclusions of all branches of knowledge. As the greatest educational philosopher of America, John Dewey has said : "The primary aim of philosophy is knowledge of 'Being' or 'Reality' which is more comprehensive, fundamental and ultimate than the knowledge which can be provided by the organs and methods at the disposal of the special sciences."[2] For this kind of an ultimate, comprehensive knowledge the first principles of physical, natural and social sciences must be the basis.

Philosophy as an Activity

Studying philosophy is just as good as engaging in an activity. Many have considered philosophy as primarily an activity or a process ; secondarily as a subject-matter for teaching and learning. As Levison defines it : "Philosophy is first of all an activity of a certain kind and only secondarily a subject-matter consisting of a definite body of literature."[3] We are engaged in numerous activities everyday. Should we call them philosophy ? If not, then in what way can we say that philosophy is an activity. Philosophy is a mental activity ; thinking about the problems of mankind. For example it is a mental activity of thinking about life, its nature and purposes ; the mind and its occupations, birth, death and other phenomena of world ; feelings, ideas, values of social life, etc. This activity must not be limited to a study and discussion among a few persons but be able to stimulate the interest of humanity at large. As Russell puts it : "Philosophy proper deals with matters of interest to the general educated public and loses much of its value if only a few professionals can understand it."[4] Henderson also has expressed himself in a similar way while defining philosophy : "Philosophy is a rigorous, disciplined, guarded analysis of some of the most difficult problems which man has ever faced."[5] If the life and works of the great philosophers is studied in the light of these definitions it can be perceived that philosophy right from the earliest times has interested itself in the common problems of mankind. The title of one of the many books by John Dewey and written purely about philosophy is 'Problems of Men'. However, Dewey argues that philosophy is not a panacea for the problems of men but is that which emerges out of the methods employed by them to solve their problems. Philosophy must emerge out of life rather than life being guided by dictates of philosophy. For Socrates, philosophy was a daily activity. He used to invite the Athenian citizens into arguments and discuss with them the problems of life and the world around without himself getting bored. That is how he was referred to as the gadfly of Athens. Therefore, philosophy can be conceived of as an activity of criticism, clarification and interpretation of life. D.J. O'Connor has defined philosophy as 'an activity of criticism or clarification.'[6] There has emerged a distinct and well known school of philosophy in the present century which has kept this meaning of philosophy as basic to their distinctiveness. This school is represented by great scholars such as Wittgenstein, Israel Scheffler, D.J. O'Connor, A.J. Ayer, P.H. Hirst and is called as "Language Analysis".

Philosophy as 'A Comprehensive Picture of the Universe'

Philosophers have attributed this meaning to philosophy right from the beginning. The Greek Philosopher Sophocles had said that a philosopher had to see life steadily and see it as a whole. He must have a holistic and self-contained view of the universe. As Henderson puts it : "Philosophy gives a synoptic view of universe."[7] It gives a total picture, a synthetic understanding, a synoptic vision and an integrated view. Keeping this meaning in his mind, Dr. Radhakrishnan has defined the aim of education thus : "The aim of education is to give an integrated view of the universe."[8] The physical, natural and social sciences might provide an integral understanding of the physical, natural and human world, but fail to offer a holistic vision of the universe. The philosopher would study generalisations of all the above sciences and on the basis of his accumulated understanding would offer an organised and systematic knowledge of the universe. As Dewey has viewed it : "with respect to subject-matter, philosophy is an attempt to comprehend—that is, gather together the varied details of the world and of life into a single inclusive whole."[9] As such philosophy does not involve the creation and publication of knowledge ; it implies a study and reorganisation of the knowledge that is already available. It involves the organisation, interpretation, clarification and criticism of what is already within the realm of the known and the experienced. It is a way of looking at knowledge which we already have. If science is defined as a systematised and organised body of knowledge then philosophy is a reorganisation of all such scientific knowledge. It is for this reason that Brubacher has called philosophy as the science of sciences.[10] It has been called as the mother of sciences because the independent disciplines of today were an integral part of philosophy at one or the other times of yester years. Plato also conceived of the philosopher as a spectator of all time and all existence.

P.G. Smith has suggested three dimensions for philosophical thinking. They are comprehensiveness, penetration and flexibility.[11] 'Flexibility' is a noteworthy dimension of philosophy. Philosophy does not offer a panacea for all problems of mankind or an eternal truth about the organisation of the universe. It will also change as the truths, view points and knowledge in the sciences, on which philosophy is based, go on changing and expanding. Philosophy does not preach an eternal and all pervasive permanent knowledge. As Kilpatrick describes it : "Philosophy is a point of view, outlook on life. The test of a good philosophy : It should stand the test of scrutiny, re-examination and revision in the light of new problems and new insights."[12] Therefore, in this way, the philosopher must possess an integrated, self-contained but flexible view of the universe.

Philosophy as a Guide to a Way of Life

Philosophy is a view of life. It gives a direction to life, offers a design for living. Dr. Radhakrishnan has suggested this meaning to philosophy through the titles of two of his works ; they are 'The Hindu view of life' and 'The Idealist view of life'. Philosophy directs life and gets refined on the basis of experiences of life. When man is caught in ambiguous situations, he thinks about morality, duty, justice, right, goodness, world and its management, etc., and reaches his own conclusions. Philosophy is created out of life's experiences and life is through the light of such philosophy. As Arnold Reid, formerly Director of the Institute of Education, London and Professor of educational philosophy has put it : "I repeat that philosophy is, in the end, about life, and not only about reported statements concerning life, and that one must live richly in order to think and talk sense."[13] Even among Indian philosophers there was not much divergence between the philosophy and the way of life For them life was the laboratory of philosophy. Gandhiji has titled his biography as *My Experiments with Truth*. Once when he was asked to give a message for the world he is reported to have answered thus : 'My life is my message' (Humanistic Idealism). It is said that philosophy in the West was born out of wonder. (Thales of Miletus has been considered by the historians of Western philosophic thought as the father of Western philosophy as he was the first to wonder about the phenomena of the world around him.) But philosophy in India emerged as a result of reflection over the experiences and problems of everyday living. Prof. Hiriyanna has also suggested the same meaning for philosophy in his writings.[14]

Philosophy and Science

There is an unique relation between philosophy and science. Philosophy takes over from the end-point of science. The zenith of science is the nadir of philosophy. Philosophy grows on the base of the detailed knowledge of science. As Butler has put it : "Both are interested in knowledge. But there is a difference in the kind of knowledge. Science seeks knowledge of facts. Philosophy seeks ultimate knowledge."[15] This fundamental knowledge though beyond the facts of science still is based on them. The following description help in understanding the relation between the two—

Phenix : "Science attempts only at the discovery of facts. Philosophy is not just interested in the discovery of facts. Rather it is interested in facts insofar as to provide an attitude towards them. It tries to organise, interpret, clarify and criticise the already discovered facts of science."[16]

Dewey : "When science denotes not simply a report of the particular facts discovered about the world but a general attitude towards it—as distinct from special things to do—it merges into philosophy."[17]

G.T.W. Patrick : "Between science and philosophy the very closest relationship exists. They spring from the same root, the love of knowledge, and they aspire to the same end, the knowledge of reality. While science describes the facts, philosophy interprets them."[18]

Brubacher : "Science is interested in the proximate or efficient causes of facts, while philosophy is concerned with its ultimate or final causes."[19]

Oxford Definition of Philosophy : "That which deals with the most general causes and principles of things."[20]

The foregone statements suggest that if the outlook of the scientist is partial, narrow in scope and detailed, the outlook of a philosopher is holistic and comprehensive. But to enrich life, for the world to trace the path of progress, philosophy and science must be complementary. For instance, science would supply the technical knowledge and skills required to generate atomic energy. There is a need for a healthy and desirable philosophy to put this energy into creative and constructive use. An unhealthy philosophy would tempt one to misuse the same energy for destructive purposes. If discovery of knowledge is the task of science, the task of philosophy is to direct the use of such knowledge. As such there is no contradiction between science and philosophy ; rather there is a harmony between the two.

Philosophy and Religion : Those who are not aware of the nature and methods of philosophy often confuse it for religion. Though there are a few similarities between the two, still there are some prominent differences. The objective of both religion and philosophy is the same—discovery of truth—for instance about the self, relation between self and the world around, etc. The difference between the two lies in the method of investigation of truth. Faith is the basis of the method in religion. Religion begins with a faith in a few *a priori* beliefs. These beliefs should not be questioned. Commitment to these beliefs on the part of the individual is a primary requisite. But the method of philosophy is an independent, objective and impartial enquiry. If philosophy is speculative and contemplative, religion is action-oriented and ritualistic. Religion is an approach to realise the given ultimate realities of life. Philosophy is an attempt to understand the ultimate realities of life. Though these distinctions apply fully in the context of Western philosophies and religions, still they do not perfectly fit in, in the context of Indian culture. This is because, the religions of India are more speculative and philosophical. As Bertrand Russell[21] and Albert Schweitzer[22] have opined, it is difficult to draw a clear line of demarcation between the religions and philosophies of India.

Problems of Philosophy

The problems studied by philosophy are classified under five divisions for purposes of systematisation. They are : Metaphysics, Epistemology, Axiology, Logic and Aesthetics. Truth about the metaphysical nature of the universe ; nature of time, space and the universe around, cause and effect relationships, the functions and nature of the mind, etc., fall under metaphysics. The nature and worthiness of knowledge, methods of knowledge, etc., fall under epistemology ; values, types of values, methods of value realisation, etc., are discussed under axiology ; nature of thought, methods of thought (*e.g.*, Bacon's inductive method and Aristotle's deductive method and recently Piaget has discovered the method of transduction), analysis of experience, etc., fall under logic ; the theory of beauty, relation between truth and beauty, etc., are discussed under aesthetics.

REFERENCES

1. Plato : 'Republic' (Tr.) B. Jowett, Section 475, in the "Dialogues of Plato", Vol. II, Clarendon Press (IV Edition), Oxford, 1953, p. 335.
2. Dewey, John : "Problems of Men". Introductory Note, p. 5, Philosophical Library, New York, 1946.
3. Levison, Arnold B : "*The uses of philosophy and the problems of Educators*" in "Selected Readings in the Philosophy of Education" (Ed.) Park Joe : Macmillan Co., New York, 1968, p. 26.
4. Russell, Bertrand : "Human Knowledge."
5. Henderson, S.V.P. : "Introduction to the Philosophy of Education", University of Chicago Press, Chicago, 1947, Chapter I, p. 4.
6. "An Introduction to the Philosophy of Education", Routledge and Kegan Paul, London, 1966, p. 1.
7. Henderson, *op. cit.*, Chapter I, p. 5.
8. University Education Commission Report, Chapter I.
9. 'Democracy and Education', Macmillan & Co., New York, 1944. p. 324.
10. Brubacher, J.S. : "Modern Philosophies of Education", Tata McGraw-Hill, New Delhi, 1969, Chapter I, p. 323.

11. "*Philosophy of Education*", Introductory studies, Harper & Row, N. Y., 1965, Chapter I, pp. 8-14.

12. "Philosophy of Education", Macmillan and Co., N. Y., 1963, Chapter I.

13. L.A. Reid : 'Philosophy and the Theory and Practice of Education', Evans Bros. Ltd., London, 1965, p. 23.

14. For example Hiriyanna, M. : "The Aim of Indian Philosophy" in 'Philosophical Studies', Kavyalaya Publishers, Mysore.

15. Butler : "Four Philosophies and their Practice in Education and Religion", Harper & Row, N. Y., 1968, p. 4.

16. Phenix : 'Philosophy of Education', Holt and Rinehart, N. Y., 1958, pp. 1 and 2.

17. Dewey : 'Democracy and Education', p. 324.

18. G.T.W. Patrick : 'Introduction to Philosophy', Allen & Unwin, London, 1958.

19. Brubacher : *op. cit.*, p. 323.

20. Shorter Oxford Dictionary.

21. Russell : "Why I am not a Christian ?" Collected Essays, Allen & Unwin, London, 1959.

22. Schweitzer : "Civilisation and Ethics", Adam and Charles Black, London, 1923, pp. 25, 30.

CHAPTER 2

Meanings of Education

Education does not have a definition of universal acceptance. There are numerous definitions of education and meanings that are suggested by these definitions. These diverse meanings correspond to the many functions of education. A study of these meanings is useful for a systematic understanding of education.

Etymological Meaning

The origin of the word 'Education' is from the Latin root 'Educare'. 'Educare' means 'to lead out or bring forth'; it implies that through organised questions the knowledge, understanding and the potentialities of children have to be brought out; it is not pouring in knowledge assuming that children are like empty vessels. Gandhiji's definition of education in the *Harijan* issue of 1937, fits into the meaning implied here : "Education is drawing out of the best in child and man—body, mind and spirit." The system of education at this time gave credence only to the intellectual development of the child and had equated education to the imparting of knowledge. That is why Gandhiji desired that the best of body and spirit also be drawn out along with that of the mind. Swami Vivekananda also has defined education in a similar way : "Education is the manifestation of the perfection that is already in man." It means that there is a 'self' in man which is self-contained and is a part of the universal reality. The purpose of education is to make man aware of this cosmic power in him and enable him to draw this out to lead a complete life.

Criticism

When education is defined as an attempt to bring out the hidden potentialities in the student and his understanding of the universe around him, then one may wonder whether the activities of our school be rightly called as education. How to bring out from children the knowledge of history, geography, literature and mathematics ? It is possible, to a limited extent, to bring out from children through appropriate questions their awareness of natural and social processes. But this meaning cannot be applied in its totality when the programme of school education is kept in view.

Education as Acquisition of Knowledge

Education is defined as acquisition of knowledge in relation to a definition of philosophy as love of knowledge. The famous Greek philosopher Socrates had said that 'knowledge is virtue' and he who is knowledgeable is virtuous and just. Francis Bacon had said that 'knowledge is power' and the knowledge of the universe around is instrumental for the progress of a society. Even in the *Bhagavad Gita* Sri Krishna has set knowledge as one of the qualifications of a *Sthithaprajna*, a person of equanimity, poise and mental balance. Hence, the concept of education as acquisition of knowledge was prevalent since the beginning of history of education till recent times. Even now such a meaning prevails in the minds of the lay public. This view of education has been very well reflected in the opening pages of Charles Dickens' 'Hard Times'. Children must be stuffed with as much knowledge as possible, because character and sound education are associated with it. Even now, one of the popular beliefs in education is that knowledge leads to wisdom.

Criticism

The concept that education is acquisition of knowledge, those who are knowledgeable are virtuous and wise is not completely true. A study of the biographies of great scholars and intellectuals in the history of mankind reveals that there are many exceptions to the belief that knowledge leads to virtue or wisdom. To illustrate, though Francis Bacon and Jean Jacqueau Rousseau were great intellectuals still their personal lives were neither wise nor virtuous. Therefore, many a times a cultured illiterate would appear superior to a knowledgeable rogue. When we look around our social environment we come across many a persons who are considered as educated on the basis of their certificates from educational institutions but behave in uncivilised, distasteful, uncultured ways and lead an unworthy and ignoble life. Can we call them educated ? Is education acquisition of knowledge ? Such questions as these would pass through our minds. Moreover, when we observe the wise ways of life, behaviours worthy of appreciation, high level of ethical discrimination of quite a few rural folk who have never seen a school, we are left wondering about the meaning of education.

Education as a Tool to Discipline the Intellect

John Locke, the English philosopher of the sixteenth century conceived of the mind as a function of different components (faculties); *e.g.*, Memory, Imagination and Thinking. The school of thinking which believes in such a concept of the mind as this is called as faculty psychology. However, the mind at the time of birth of the child will be like a clean slate, as Locke described it a 'tabula rasa'. He believed that the different faculties of the mind grow as a result of respective and successive stimulation from the surrounding world. Therefore, mental development means the development of these different faculties. Children's mind is just like plastic and it is pliable. It is just like a twig. It will grow in the direction you bend it. Therefore, education means the training of the different faculties of the mind. For *e.g.*, thinking can be developed through the teaching of geometry, memory can be developed through the teaching of history.

Criticism

Locke's concept of the mind is not accepted either by contemporary philosophy or psychology. The child's mind is not a clean slate on which anything can be scribbled ; rather the child brings to the school its congenital or hereditary gifts and his experiences of the external world around him. Education which does not recognise either the in-born abilities or the carried over experiences of children is of no value at all.

Education as a Preparation for Life

Every individual desires to live a successful life. If life has to be successful, the skills and the ability to conveniently solve the problems of life has to be acquired. For example, may be according to some people, an individual needs to be healthy, to be employed, married and be knowledgeable as to how to bring up children, conduct himself in a peaceful and co-operative way with other members of society, and live as an efficient and worthy citizen of democracy ; then his life may be said to be successful. In trying to realise this successful life he would be facing many problems. He needs certain type and amount of knowledge, skills, attitudinal framework and behaviours which are necessary to solve his problems of life and realise the successful or complete life. Therefore, children must be familiarised with the problems of adult life and the solutions therein when they are studying in school. In this sense education is a preparation for life. The famous biologist and educationist of the nineteenth centruy in England, Herbert Spencer conceived of education in this fashion. The influence of Spencer on the second half of the nineteenth century England was profound.

Criticism

If education is conceived of as a preparation for life then the period of preparation and consequently the experiences, needs, interests and aspirations of pupils during that time become secondary. Such education ignores the developmental rhythms and life-space of children, hence becomes irrelevant and unreal. This view is adult-centred and not child-centred. According to contemporary trends in educational thinking life itself is a process of education ; from womb to tomb, birth to death, cradle to grave, it is believed that we are being educated.

Education as Direction

Human infants are born with a number of unlearned responses, natural tendencies, impulses, urges and drives. These natural impulses, if left unchecked and uncontrolled, would lead to a barbarian way of life. A life that is left to the self-direction of nature would be disorganised, unsystematic, purposeless and unprincipled. On the other hand, a life that is subject to the controls of social life would be systematic, principled and purposeful. Therefore, it is necessary to refine the natural impulses. These natural impulses may be observed in all individuals irrespective of caste, class, language, religion and nationality. But the method of refinement, control and gratification of natural impulses varies from group to group. The explanation for the diverse cultures of the world can be traced to the different methods of refinement. John Dewey opines that the natural or naive impulses of the individuals do not agree with the life-customs of their group. The refinement of these naive impulses or in other words modification of natural development is education.

'Modification' implies direction. As such refinement of natural tendencies needs direction. Direction has got two steps. They are : Control and Guidance.

Control

Control denotes the process by which an individual is impressed upon to subordinate his natural impulses to public or group interests. It is not physical but intellectual. As Dewey feels : "Because the activities of children today are controlled by selected and charged stimuli, children are able to traverse in a short time what the race has needed slow, tortured ages to attain."[1]

Guidance

Guidance is the act of carrying children towards predetermined goals after their natural impulses are controlled.

As such direction involves both control and guidance. But what kind of direction characterises education ? As

Phenix would answer the question : "Education is the process whereby persons intentionally guide the development of persons."[2] It would be useful to analyse the above definition of education.

(*a*) Persons guide persons. As it is a person-to-person relationship, education is a human enterprise. In fact, Sir John Adams has described education as a bi-polar process :

Educator←———→Educand

(Stimulus)←——→(Response)

(*b*) Then, it is a process. It means that education is not limited to any particular period of life but is a continuous activity.

(*c*) The result of this process is development *e.g.*, the development of social consciousness.

(*d*) Another special feature of this process is that here guidance is not mechanical and blind but intentional, purposive or deliberate. To illustrate, the guidance given by a policeman stationed in the centre of a bottleneck of traffic is mechanical as he is not interested in the destination of the commuter.

Criticism

This meaning of education is naive and abstract. It does not concretely and operationally specify the ends and nature of direction. From a practical standpoint of school organisation, this meaning is not of much value.

Education as Growth

The meaning of education is representative of the educational thought of John Dewey, the great philosopher and educationist of America. Dewey defines education thus : "Since growth is the characteristic of life, education is all one with growing, it has no end beyond itself."[3] Dewey's definition may be explained with the help of the following diagram :

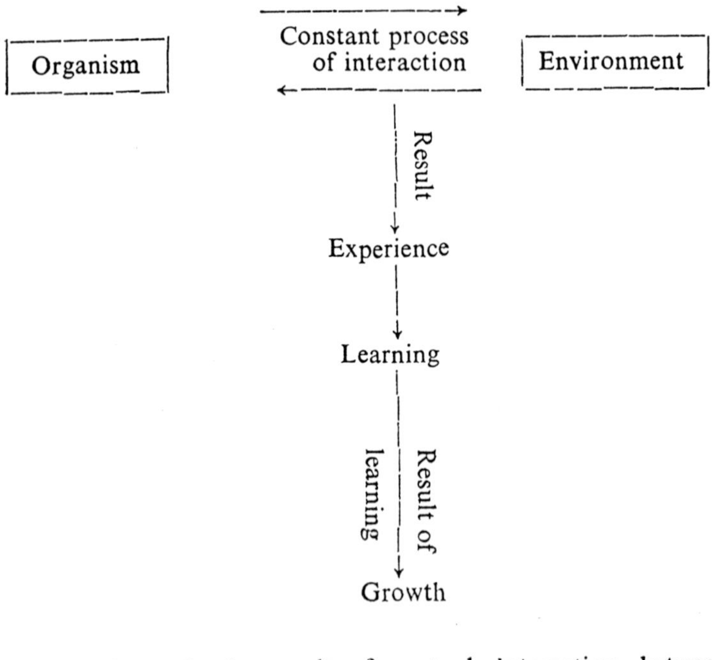

Experience is the result of mutual interaction between the organism and the environment. Though all experience results in learning still all learning is a product of experience. Development is effected by learning. The entire process of growth and development which is caused by learning from experience is called *Education*. To apply to the school situation, the child brings its own experiences to the school. Education is the reconstruction of these experiences. Dewey has given a 'technical definition of education' as follows :

"It is that reconstruction or re-organisation of experience which adds to the meaning of experience, and which increases ability to direct the course of subsequent experience."[4]

Analysis of the above definition :

a priori assumption : the child has his own experiences, then, education :

(*a*) reconstructs these experiences or reorganises them, refines them and gives a meaning to them.

(*b*) this reconstruction, that is (*a*), adds to the refinement and meaning of further experiences ;

(*c*) (*a*) and (*b*) together develop the ability in the child to control and direct the subsequent experiences.

Two illustrations follow which would help to understand the above definition.

I. Children will have seen the sun, the stars and the universe around them :

(*a*) Using these experiences, lesson on solar system may be given;

(*b*) (*a*) would be useful when children have to learn about the cosmic order or the universe around them;

(*c*) (*a*) and (*b*) would be helpful for a self-study of calendars and eclipses.

II. Children in rural (urban) areas will have witnessed a number of social processes.

(*a*) These experiences can be utilised to teach about the problems of rural life.

(*b*) (*a*) would be useful in learning about national problems.

(*c*) (*a*) and (*b*) would be useful for children in attempting to solve rural and national problems.

Growth of the child is a process which comprises all these stages ; growth is the end-product of education. Let us understand the concept of growth as Dewey conceives it.

What is Growth ? : Growth is a cumulative movement of directed action. It is an all-round-physical intellectual, social and emotional—development[5] of the potentialities of an individual. Such a development must be inter-related, interdependent, organised, harmonious and a product of directed activities.

When is Growth Possible ? : The primary condition of growth is immaturity. Immaturity does not imply the absence of power to grow but means the ability to develop, the power to grow and the possibility for growth. It is a positive quality in the child. There are two characteristics for immaturity. They are :

(*a*) dependence and (*b*) plasticity.

Dependence

Compared to the infants of animals, human infants are largely helpless in adjusting themselves to the physical environment around them. The infants of animals are born with a number of physical endowments. They are able to look after themselves immediately after they are born or within a short span of time. In this respect, human infants are dependent on others. As time passes the child grows from dependence to independence or self-dependence. Arnold Toynbee's criterion of growth in the context of national life is equally applicable to individual life. "The criterion of growth is progress towards self-determination."[6] However, the dependence of the human infant on adult is not a defect or a weakness. From a social standpoint, dependence denotes a power as it involves interdependence between the child and the society. Human infants can get along with physical incapacity just because of their social capacity. For instance, a child learns the first lessons of love in the laps of his mother. Interdependence is only through dependence. The child develops healthy attitudes towards social life only through dependence. Therefore, one of the chief characteristics of growth is progress from dependence to self-reliance and development of a healthy attitude towards interdependence.

Plasticity

"Plasticity is the capacity to retain and carry over from prior experience factors which modify subsequent activities."[7] Plasticity is the capacity to learn from experiences, the ability to develop flexible dispositions ; it is an ability to learn from experiences in such a way as to assist in the direction of future activities. It refers to the openness of the mind to learn and relearn from experiences. Education of the mind is possible so long as it retains the quality of plasticity. The ability and the mental set to adjust to the precarious situations of life must be developed through education. Education must develop the habit of adjustment.

Growth is a consequence of the adjustment caused by learning characterised by plasticity. Therefore, growth is the end-product of education. When growth is equated with education, it does not refer to a partial growth but an integral or all-round growth of the individual such as the physical, social, intellectual and emotional aspects. In this sense, education is an all-round, integrated growth ; and growth is the characteristic of life. As education is also characterised by growth, life itself is education.

Criticism

Among those who were influenced by Dewey's concept of 'Education as life', Kilpatrick, Childs and Ratner were prominent. Under their leadership, in the beginning of this century, a movement called as the 'progressive education movement'[8] became very popular. However, after the two World Wars, this concept of education and the American system of education based on this concept came into pungent criticism; it was especially so after Soviet Russia launched its Sputnik for the first time in 1958. The main points of criticism are : it is inconceiveable that there can be no goals of education, as Dewey believed, beyond growth. Growth is only a process ; and every process must have an aim. Even from a practical stand-point it is almost impossible to conceive of an education without goals. Even growth must have aims. Theodore Brameld, George S. Counts and Harry S. Broudy are only a few names who were critical of this concept of education. Of them, George Counts attacked severely the progressive schools in one of his influential writings : "Dare the schools build a new social order ?"

Education as Transmission of Culture

The meanings of education discussed so far have individual as their focus. But from the view point of the welfare of a society, education means the transmission of culture. It is a platitude to say that man is born *with* a biological heritage *into* a social heritage. Culture is another name for this social heritage. In a subtle way, the essence of all human achievements is culture. In the words of E.B. Tylor : "Culture is that '*complex whole*' which includes knowledge, beliefs, art, morals, law, custom and any other capabilities and habits acquired by man as a member of society."[9] This culture is transmitted by every society to its next generation in the interests of the stability and continuity of the society. Education is the process of cultural transmission. J.S. Mill has defined education referring to this meaning : "Education is the culture which each generation purposely gives to those who are to be its successors, in order to qualify them for at least keeping up, and if possible for raising, the level of improvement which has been maintained."[10] Two points have to be noted in the above definition.

(*a*) Preservation of culture is possible only through education. The goal of all activities of every generation is the preservation of culture. For example, the life of Indian culture is in the hands of its youth. If they ignore or overlook the glory of their culture and begin to imitate another culture, it will be detrimental to the present progress of India.[11]

(*b*) There is no culture which can be said to be perfect. There is a need to refine it. For instance, though Indian culture has a hoary past, is one of the great illustrations of ancient cultures, is claimed to be timeless, still a number of customs which have grown with it over time such as the caste system, untouchability and child-marriage need refinement.[12] Similarly there is a need to refine the techniques of production and technology of agriculture. Such refinements have to be brought about through education only.

Just as an individual insures his life so that his dependents may not suffer after his exit from this world, similarly the elders of a society insure the stability, security and welfare of their younger generations through education. They would see to it that the younger generation will not suffer after they pass away. Hence, education is transmission of culture. Need for sequential inter-linkages between Education and Culture in the development of a child's personality has been adequately highlighted in Chapter XXI of the Programme of Action of the New Education Policy, 1986.

Criticism

Such a concept of education immediately receives universal acceptance. However, as a footnote to Mill's definition it may be added that transmission of culture is only a function of education and not its purpose. The purpose of education is the growth of culture.[13] There is a new movement in American philosophical thinking in education known as 'Reconstructionism' which attempts to reconstruct the culture of the world through education. Theodore Brameld is the exponent of this school.

RELATION BETWEEN PHILOSOPHY AND EDUCATION

The relation that education bears to philosophy depends on the meaning attributed to philosophy. As such there can be multiple approaches to the determination of the relation between the two as there are multiple meanings of philosophy. However, if philosophy is taken to be a determiner of the constitutents of a worthy way of life education then becomes a means to inculcate that worthy way of life. In other words philosophy determines the ends, goals or aims of life and education is an attempt to realise these goals. It is again difficult to define concretely as to what constitutes a worthy way of life. It may be a life of harmony with nature, one of social service, union with the External, democratic citizenship, economic independence, etc. These may individually or collectively or in any permutations be taken as the goals of life. In terms of national dimensions it may be communism, capitalism, socialism, democracy, dictatorship or a combination of any of them. As such in India socialistic, secular democracy is the nation's philosophy. Under any of these circumstances education is only a means to realise the end. The ends are set by philosophy and there are as many conflicting and complementary ends as there are philosophies. As Henderson put it : "Educational aims cannot be determined apart from the ends and aims of life itself for educational aims grow out of life's aims. To determine what constitutes worth living has been one of the chief tasks of philosophy."[14] Earlier T.P. Nunn also had said that "Educational aims are correlative to ideals of life."[15] Ideals of life vary and educational aims vary correspondingly. Philosopher studies all the available information about man and the universe in which he lives and then with this knowledge as his nucleus and base, speculates about the nature, origin, purpose and destiny of man. He interprets the available knowledge in the light of his perceptions and draws his own conclusions about the goals of individual and social life. The educator enables the educands to realise the defined goals. That is why, philosophy is said to be the contemplative or speculative side and education the dynamic or active side of life. Sir John Adams had said that education is the dynamic side of philosophy. Philosophy and education are two sides of the same coin—life. It is a relation similar to the one between the planner and policy-maker and the executive officer. As Ross puts it "Education is the active aspect of philosophical belief, the practical means of realising ideals of life."[16] Philosophical outlook proceeds educational effort and educational effort prcceeds from philosophical outlook.

As considered by a few thinkers education plays a role which is far more than that of an agent or a means. Education in a sense, is a testing ground of ideas. Ideas about the goals of life are tested for their practicability through education. Theory may be a guide to practice but practice also offers correctives to theory. Such a dynamic relation between philosophy and education was visualised by John Dewey. For him this relation is so intense that he considers philosophy as the general theory of education.[17]

VALUES OF THE STUDY OF EDUCATIONAL PHILOSOPHY

The values of the study of educational philosophy for any educational practitioner—classroom teacher, headmaster, inspector of schools, educational administrator, educational planner and policy-maker, guidance counsellor, educational researcher and the like—are numerous and manifold. It is easier to internalise the values from a study of the subject than to verbalise and to decipher in terms of tangible outcomes and specifications. However, an attempt to describe the values will not be futile.

The study of educational philosophy gives a sense of 'meaning' to the educational practitioner for his work and its place in the general scheme of life. It enables him to see clearly the relationship between his day-to-day, so-called routine work and the goals of individual, social and national life. He will not feel that he is lost in the wilderness counting the trees without having an idea of the horizons. It would help him to adjust himself to his work to fit in as a square peg and if necessary to try to change in his own possible ways the *status quo*. Such an awareness would give him a purpose and a direction to his life which he would be able to infuse in his children or teachers or executives as the case may be.

It enables the educational practitioner to interpret his professional experiences in the light of theoretical perceptions and *vice versa*. As such he would be able to identify inconsistencies and eliminate conflicts and contradictions in the theory and practice of education. It would provide him with a conceptual framework for action.

It is also hoped that by a study of educational philosophy the educational practitioner would be able to develop a critical attitude in life. By an intelligent handling of the subject the teacher can develop such an attitude. The author has taught the subject for quite a few years. When he used to present different schools of philosophy and their implications to education or discuss problems such as freedom *Vs* authority in education, Nationalism *Vs* Internationalism, Individual *Vs* Social aims of education etc., invariably students both at the graduate and post-graduate levels used to complain to him that they were confused about the choice of a school of philosophy or in deciding the degree of freedom to be given to children and the authority to be exercised over them, etc.

Then the author's reply used to be 'my purpose of teaching, has been realised' because 'I wanted to confuse you, as confusion is the beginning of all self-learning' and confusion leads to critical thinking. Critical thinking is the means of philosophical enquiry. The development of critical thinking in the educational practitioner about problems of education and the consequent filter-effects on those who come under his influence need no additional emphasis.

Educational Philosophy and Schools : The study of educational philosophy has an added significance for those who are concerned with the management of schools such as teachers, headmasters, supervisors and correspondents. By a study of metaphysics, teleology, etc., and their implications to education they would be, it is hoped, able to answer to themselves such questions as (*a*) what kind of social outlook they are supporting ? (*b*) what kind of social outlook they ought to support ?

Curriculum is the student's avenue of knowledge. It is necessary to understand the elements of the curriculum or the nature of such knowledge. The study of epistemology and its implications to education would be of immense benefit in this regard.

Education is said to be an attempt at the development of a scale of values in children. To understand the meaning, nature and relative importance of the values of life a study of axiology and its implications to education would be most fruitful. Similarly the study of other branches of philosophy such as aesthetics and logic have their own values in organising aesthetic experiences for children and develop critical thinking in them.

The discussion of the values of the study of educational philosophy to educational practitioner and the schools and the examples drawn are only illustrative and suggestive but not exhaustive.

The 'schools' approach to philosophy of education is widely followed in the Indian Universities. In the last two decades, new approaches to the subject are observed in the Western Universities and Institutions. Issues and problems in education are discussed in a philosophical and theoretical perspective rather than within a standardised framework of schools. For developments in England in the past 30 years (1952-82) one may refer to the 30th anniversary issue of the *British Journal of Educational Studies* Vol. 30, Number 1. An illuminating review article is there by R.F. Dearden on 'Philosophy of Education'. Incidently Dearden is also the author of 'Philosophy of Primary Education.'

REFERENCES

1. Dewey : "Democracy and Education", Macmillan, N.Y., 1944, p. 37.
2. Phenix : "Philosophy of Education", *op. cit.*, p. 13.
3. *Ibid.*, p. 53.
4. *Ibid.*, p. 76.
5. *Note* : Psychologists draw a number of distinctions between growth and development, but such distinctions are technical and do not apply to Dewey's conceptual framework.
6. "A Study of History", OUP 1947, p. 208.
7. Dewey : "Democracy and Education", p. 46.
8. For details about progressive education, refer to.
9. 'Primitive Cultures', Vol. I, Harper & Brothers, New York, 1958.
10. J.S. Mill : "On Education".
11. K.M. Munshi : "Foundations of Indian Culture", Bhavan's Publications, would be a useful reader, p. 133.
12. K.M. Panikkar: "Essential Features of Indian Culture", Bhavan's Publications, would be a useful reader.
13. D.J. O' Connor : "An Introduction to Philosophy of Education", Routledge & Kegan Paul, London, 1957, p. 7.
14. Henderson : "Introduction to Philosophy of Education". The University of Chicago Press, Chicago, 1947, pp. 16-17.
15. Nunn, T P : "Education, Its Data and First Principles". The Modern Educators Library Series, Edward Arnold & Co., London, 1920, p. 2.
16. Ross : "Groundwork of Educational Theory", George G. Haraff & Co. Ltd., London, 1958, p. 16.
17. 'Democracy and Education', Macmillan and Co., N. Y., 1965, p. 330.

CHAPTER 3

Naturalism in Education

Exponents[1] : In so far as the history of Western Philosophy is concerned Naturalism is the oldest philosophy. Philosophy in the West is supposed to have begun with 'wonder'. Man wondered about the phenomenon of his existence. A number of changes in the physical universe were observed then as they are observed even to this day. There was an attempt to find out the residual permanent substance that underlies all change in the environment. Thales of Miletus, 7th century B.C., who is considered as the father of Western philosophy found his final substance within nature. In the following centuries there lived a chain of other Greek thinkers, prominent among them being Leucippus and Democritus (5th century B.C.), Epicurus (341-270 B.C.) and Lucretius (1st century B.C.) who were all called atomists because they conceived of reality as fundamentally composed of atoms. As such they also discovered reality within nature. Down through the ages there have been naturalist strains of thought. Some of the eminent philosophers and social reformers like Thomas Hobbes (1588-1679), Jean Jaequeau Rousseau (1712-1778) and Herbert Spencer (1820-1903) were also naturalists. Even in ancient India there sprang up a system of philosophy known as the Charvaka School which may be called as the naturalistic philosophy of India. Brhaspathi was a great exponent of this philosophy.

MAIN PHILOSOPHICAL IDEAS OF NATURALISM

One of the main concerns in which a student of philosophy of education must be interested about a school of philosophy is its idea of reality. Naturalists believe that nature is the ultimate reality and is propelled by her own laws and consequently determined by them. For them reality and nature are identical. They have no belief in a supernatural reality. As Hocking writes : "Naturalism denies the existence of anything beyond nature, behind nature, other than nature, such as the supernatural or other-worldly."[2] If they are asked : "What causes nature ?", their answer is "Nature is the total system of causes. To ask for a cause of nature, outside of nature, a 'First Cause', 'a God', 'an ultimate cause' is meaningless."

Another significant issue that distinguishes one school from another is the concept of the mind. As naturalists do not believe in anything that is spiritual they do not make a distinction between mind and body (matter). This position of the naturalist is in contradiction to that of the idealists for whom the 'mind' is spiritual (as that can conceive of ideas which alone are real) and the body is just matter which is perishable and through which the mind manifests. Because man has mind, for idealists man is spiritual in essence. But for the naturalists man is also matter and his mind is the result of his brain-function. As an evidence for their position naturalists cite quite a few experiments wherein certain parts of the cerebrum which were associated with certain functions of the mind such as memory, perception, etc., were electronically controlled, the subject lost those powers of the mind. As such the mind as a function of the brain which is matter is not different from matter.

One of the other main concerns of philosophical enquiry which has a bearing on the principles and practices of education is epistemology or the theory of knowledge. The fundamental question that has been raised time and again in the history of philosophical thought which has a direct relation to curriculum theory and practice is "What knowledge is of most worth ?" The naturalists in answer to this question would highlight the value of scientific knowledge as of utmost worth. Herbert Spencer, (who may be considered as the doyen of science education and similarly a great scientist) said that scientific knowledge must be the context of living. Even Francis Bacon had emphasised that empirical and experimental knowledge was worthy of acquisition.

The method of acquiring knowledge advocated by the naturalists is the inductive method ; it is the method of science. It involves the following stages : meticulous observation (of data), exhaustive collection, careful classification, accurate description, intelligent interpretation and cautioned generalisation. Francis Bacon is considered to be the father of the inductive method. So naturalists believe that knowledge gained primarily through observation (not through intuition) is of utmost worth. They would like to see nature as it is, make specific observations, accumulate and then generalise about the world inductively. They do not like to deduce from generalities.

Another significant realm of philosophy where the naturalist position is distinct from other schools is axiology or the theory of value. Naturalists have no belief in spiritual values. They believe that values are resident in nature. To realise the values of nature one has to live in harmony with nature. For example, one has to avoid physical pain and suffering (especially that may be caused through meditation) as they are not natural. In other words the *summum bonum* or the highest good for them is the most abiding and refined pleasure. Pleasure is the be-all and end-all of life.

For naturalists man is basically an off-spring of nature and not a segment of society. They would not agree with the pragmatists who say that man is a social animal. Therefore, social values need to be for the good of the individuals who live in society.

NATURALISM IN EDUCATION

Need for Education : One of the basic questions that each school seeks to answer is 'why should children be educated ?' For naturalists, education is a *natural necessity* because of the long period of infancy of the child and its consequent dependence on adults. The child needs sustained protection and guidance almost throughout two decades. The offsprings of other animals such as the chicken, the calf, the baby elephant, the puppy, etc., will have negligible periods of infancy whereas the human offspring requires a few years to perform simple functions of day-to-day living. As compared to other animals man is a greatly retarded creature in his rate and manner of maturation. Education is necessary because of the prolonged infancy of man.

Meaning of Education : For naturalists, education is a process of development of the natural life. As Monroe perceives it : "Education is the process of development into an enjoyable,[3] rational, harmoniously balanced, useful and hence natural life."[4] It is interesting to mark the adjectives used behind natural life. The process of development must be natural and integrated. Education is for both body and mind ; the whole being of the child must be unfolded as an unit. As Ross puts it : "Education is merely the fostering of natural development, and true education takes place when the nature, power and inclinations of the child are allowed to develop freely with a minimum of guidance."[5] The dictum of naturalist education is "*Follow Nature*" of the pupil and of the environment as the personality of the child is fashioned by both. As such they dismiss artificial education which does not suit the nature of the child. Naturalists prefer a well organised rural education, rooted in rural atmosphere, utilising the rural resources to an inefficiently organised, ill-equipped undifferentiated education in rural areas.[6] An eminent naturalist educator Rousseau likes to look at the child as he is than as he would be. Children are not adults in the making. Therefore, education is not so much a preparation for life as life itself.[7] As Rousseau pleads : "What is to be thought of, therefore, of that cruel education which sacrifices the present to an uncertain future, that burdens a child with all sorts of restrictions and begins by making him miserable, in order to prepare him for some far-off happiness which he may never enjoy ?"[8] Therefore, an education which is in harmony with the order of natural development can stimulate the child's response to adult guidance effectively.

Aims of Education : The exposition of aims of naturalist education has been well made by Herbert Spencer.[9] He has systematically and elaborately discussed it in his work 'On Education'. The aim of education is according to Herbert Spencer, to enable the individual to lead a 'complete life'. It is the general aim which comprises of five specific objectives. These objectives must be the guiding posters of education. They are as follows :

(*a*) *Self-preservation* : The child must be able to preserve and protect his body since it is as important as the mind. He must know how to be clear and healthy himself and keep his surroundings clean. He needs to know the laws of health and hygiene—both physical and mental.

(*b*) *Securing the Necessities of Life*, that is, Education must enable an individual to develop economic efficiency.

(*c*) *Upbringing Children* : Educators must know how to nurse children and discipline them. In later life they must prove to be successful parents.

(*d*) *Maintenance of Social and Political Relations* : Education must develop in children the qualities of citizenship and equip them for effective social and political action.

(*e*) *Enjoyment of Leisure* : Life is not a serious struggle wherein one has to keep oneself physically strong, earn a living, be a responsible parent and an earnest citizen. Complete living also includes freedom from struggle to gratify one's tastes and feelings. The purpose of life is to be happy. Not only should education be pleasurable but it should help the children to lead a life of pleasure. This pleasure should not be momentary but one that is lasting and permanent. As such the system of education should provide for the proper use of leisure.

Of the five specific objectives that go to make up for the general aim 'complete living' it may be observed that except 'maintenance of social and political relations' the others are directed towards the welfare of the individual as an unit, and the exception, towards his social efficiency. As such the author feels that the often heard criticism that naturalists had no social perspective is false and unfair.

Moreover the five specific objectives are very much related

to an individual's life. To cite a few questions of common experience in social life which bring out this relation : It is common knowledge that when one meets another the usual habitual question is 'How are you ?', and when a person comes of age 'what are you doing ?', still further 'How are your children ?', 'What are they doing ?', 'What is your pastime ?', etc. An individual will be judged for the degree of his happiness and welfare on the basis of answers to these questions and judged later for his social efficiency on the basis of the quality of his social life and political consciousness. As such Spencer's delineation of the objectives of education which reflects his analysis of the requirements of an effective and successful individual and social life is one of the most systematic expositions of educational objectives in the history of educational thought.

Naturalism and the Pupil : The naturalists look at the child as a little animal.[10] Therefore, his first requirement is to be a healthy and vigorous animal able to stand the wear and tear of living. He depends upon others for his physical nourishment and mental nurture during his infancy, childhood and adolescence.

The infant educates himself to a great extent. His education should be based upon his spontaneous activities. His impromptu activities are the guides of his education. What the child likes to do is an important index to the kind of activity which is educative for him at a given stage of development. Education should be attauned to natural rhythms. Growth and development of the child follow unique rhythms and they are the sure guides to sound educational activity. This position of the naturalist is very well testified by a number of researchers in recent times in the field of developmental psychology. Working almost contemporaneously and spread over the world, developmental psychologists such as Jean Piaget, Gessel, Hurlock, Jersield, Susan Issacs, Kohlberg and others have discovered in their samples that there is an order and pattern, a rhythm in the growth and development of children. A study of all these findings would reveal that children all the world over irrespective of caste, race, colour and nationality follow, with negligible variation, a similar rhythm of development. The findings of these researchers is one of the bases of modern curriculum theory and practice.

The child is very important in the system of naturalist education. He is the centroid of the educational system. It is the child himself rather than the educator, the school, the text-book or the subject of study that is the focus of educational activity. Education should be geared to the needs of the child. The famous adage is that teachers do not teach subjects, they teach pupils. It may not strike excitement during this stage of educational history, but when it was made and popularised it did so as education before the twentieth century had different foci at different stages. In the eighteenth and nineteenth centuries subject mastery was the ideal of education. This is ironically very well reflected in the opening pages of one of Dickens' novels also.[11]

Naturalists would look at the child as a child and not as a small adult. Nature, they say, would like to have them as children and not as little adults. Therefore, educational activities should be anchored in the child's experiences and needs and not guided by the ideals of adult life.[12] As Monroe puts it : "Education finds its *purpose*, its *process* and the *means* wholly within the child's life and child's experience."[13] The 'purpose' is based on the child's interests, needs and capabilities, 'process' based on his process of growth and development, 'means' based on his activities. This attitude of holding the child as the focus of educational activity is called as the '*paidocentric attitude*' by Dr. G. Stanley Hall as referred to by Sir John Adams.[14]

Child should be given a negative education instead of a positive education. Positive education attempts to mould the child disregarding his natural inclinations. Negative education is not idleness. As Rousseau describes : "It does not give him virtue, it protects from vice ; it does not inculcate truth, it protects from error."[15] It helps the child to discover things by himself.

NATURALISM AND THE CURRICULUM

The naturalists conceive of the curriculum under two stages—earlier stage and later stage. In the earlier stage they prefer to give sensory training as they believe that senses are the gateways of knowledge and the key to experiences. Sensory training is an essential and integral part of the modern pre-school education movement. The Montessori[16] schools through their didactic apparatus and the kindergarten schools through Froebel's[17] 'gifts' provide for sensory training.

At the later stages, naturalists would like to include in the curriculum such subjects as physiology, physical and natural sciences, so much of mathematics and languages as is necessary to understand the above subjects, psychology of child development, social studies, anatomy, etc. The subjects of the curriculum reflect the five specific objectives of complete living.

NATURALISM AND METHODS OF TEACHING

Naturalistic methods of teaching emerged out of a revolt against the old, traditional and bookish methods of teaching. The child had little role in the teaching-learning process. Naturalists believe that exhaustive observation is essential for effective learning. Methods of teaching should be inductive. They advise the teachers to *tell* the child as little as possible and allow him to *discover* as much as possible. All learning should be through inductive discovery. As Butler puts it : "If the learning intellect is to be guided to its appropriate food, children must master the art of independent observation and direct acquaintance."[18] The emphasis in methods of teaching is on direct experience. Rousseau had emphatically protested against the education of his times thus : *"Give your scholar no Verbal lessons ; he should be taught by experience alone."*[19] At another place he had said "Burn the books[20] and break the walls. Throw the child into the bounty of nature."[21] All knowledge must emerge out of actual situations and experiences. Observation and experimentation should replace the chalk and talk methods. They advocate the method of self-education or auto-education.

The play-way method of teaching is advocated by naturalists. It should be noted here that the stress is on 'way' and not 'play' in the word 'play-way'. All learning should take place in the spirit of and by the method of play because play reveals the child's nature and the lines of his natural development. Play is the nature's mode of education.

One may wonder that this method of education is very slow. Naturalists would reply that educators should practice the 'art' of delay. They must not be in a haste and hurry as by doing so they ignore and contradict the natural rhythms of development. Delay helps for discovering these rhythms and provides the opportunity for joining hands with maturation. Maturation should always be encouraged.

Naturalism and the School : Naturalism attaches less importance to formal schools and text-books. Allowing that a school is necessary, then such a school should be as follows : "School should fit the child rather than to make the child fit the school" (A.S. Neill in England experimented with such a school known as the Summerhill School). The school should renounce traditional discipline, abstain from direction and give complete freedom for children. There should be no moral training or religious instruction. It must let the children to be what they are and like to be.

The character of the teaching-learning process in the school should be guided by the make-up of the learner. School life should conform to the natural processes of growth and development of children. For this, the subjects of study and methods of teaching should be rooted in the interests of children as evidenced by their spontaneous activity. School can then become an instrument of generating happiness in children.

School should cater to the varied and different interests of children. In other words, it should provide for individual differences.

School should practice the system of co-education in order to provide for natural surroundings. This helps to develop healthy sex-attitudes. Questions on sex should be openly discussed. There should be no moral taboos on free mixing of boys and girls.

Naturalism and Discipline : Naturalists advocate a free-discipline. They disapprove the practice of punishment to children. According to them punishment should be determined by natural consequences of wrong deeds ; just as children are taught in accordance with the rhythms of nature, so they should be punished as nature punishes. Punishment should be tempered with sympathy. If the child breaks the window-pane of his room, as Rousseau imagines Emile to do, it should not be punished physically. Allow the child to suffer the cold for a night so that he learns through the consequence. The proverb, 'a burnt child dreads fire' very well fits in as an illustration of nature's punishment. But a margin is left in the case of extremely dangerous circumstances. The spirit behind free discipline is that the child must learn, through a process of trial and error, by his own mistakes. The school should be organised as a free and natural society. The children should learn about the rights and duties of citizenship through participation in such a society and not through lectures.

Naturalism and the Teacher : The place of the teacher in a naturalist school is behind the scenes. His duty is just to observe the child rather than to pour information, ideas and ideals or mould character. He has to set the stage, supply the learning materials and opportunities, provide an ideal environment and create conditions under which natural development takes place.

As the method of education involves intelligent direction, the teacher should help pupils to select such experiences which contribute to growth and contain potentialities for further growth. Learning experiences should be selected, organised and co-ordinated. In fact, the teacher in the Montessori and such other nursery schools is called as a director/directress.

A teacher is not a positive but a negative educator. He is a mere observer. He should be one among children and not make his presence felt. He should not be like 'The Village School Master' described by Goldsmith :

"Well the boding tremblers had learned to trace
The day's disaster in his morning face."

As Ross describes : "So refusing all superiority, never expecting deference, the educator must be content to be regarded as an equal by equals, seeking not his own, but always giving himself. His own life is and ought to be one long give."[22]

Assessment of Naturalism : The chief strength of naturalism is its simplicity. The phenomenon of life and the world around is so confusing that there is a need to see in it an order and design which naturalism provides. It does not complicate the perception of existence by using abstract concepts.

Naturalism has to be highly regarded for its contribution to educational practice. All the recent advances in educational method which are based on child's nature have to be traced back to the influence of Naturalistic thinking.[23] Naturalistic methods of education are highly psychological as they are based on the growth and development of the child, his interests and needs, his aptitudes and activities.

Naturalism has been criticised more than it deserves to be. One of the criticisms against the school is about its belief in the saintliness of nature. Critics say that nature is not all rhythm and harmony following which man can find benefit and peace as naturalists believe it to be. Complete subordination to nature is not good. Nature has penalties to exact just as it has benefits to offer. Nature needs to be controlled.

Another criticism against naturalism is that it is metaphysically insufficient. As Ross opines : "It is in educational ideals, not in methods that naturalism fails to satisfy."[24]

The belief of naturalism that all children are capable of profiting from direct experiences and from unbridled freedom of expression is a negation of 'individual differences'. All children cannot be equated on intelligence and temperament. It implies a faith in trial and error learning to the utter neglect of other forms of learning such as through insight and conditioning. However, the role of naturalism in the realisation of the need for a humane treatment of children can never be ignored.

REFERENCES

1. The classification of philosophers into different schools is not rigid. It is quite possible that a philosopher's name can appear in more than one school because of his differing views in the areas of philosophy such as metaphysics, epistemology, axiology, aesthetics, logic, etc.

2. W.E. Hocking : "Types of philosophy" Charles Scribner's Sons, N.Y., 1959, p. 25.

3. Children must be happy to come to school. It is strange to observe that children will bear a resigned countenance when they come to school and by the end of the day are found to run away, like rats left out of a big maize shouting with joy.

4. Monroe : "A Text Book in the History of Education."

5. Ross : "Groundwork of Educational Theory."

6. It is saddening to note that sophisticated science is being taught in many rural schools without laboratories.

7. Here there is a difference between the position of Rousseau from another naturalist, Herbert Spencer, which will be clear in the discussion of aims.

8. Rousseau : 'Emile', Everyman's Library, Dent, London, (tr.) Barbara, 1914, pp. 42-43.

9. Spencer, Herbert : "*On Education*" (Ed) Andreas M. Kazamias, Classics in Education Series No. 30, Teacher's College Record, Columbia University, N.Y., 1966, p. 218.

10. Spencer : *op. cit.*

11. Dickens, Charles : 'Hard Times'.

12 Here one may observe that Spencer's outline of objectives is guided by ideals of adult life which may appear to be an anomaly in naturalist thought.

13. Monroe : "A Text Book in the History of Education", pp. 71-72.

14. Sir John Adams : "Modern Developments in Educational practice", University of London Press, London, 1928.

15. Rousseau : *op. cit.*, p. 57.

16. Montessori : "Montessori Method", Vols. I and II, William Heineman, London, 1918.

17. Froebel : "A selection from his writings" by Irene M. Lilly, Cambridge University Press, Cambridge, 1967, p. 69.

18. Butler, J. Donald : "Four Philosophies and their Practice in Education and Religion", (III Ed.), Harper & Row, New York, 1968, p. 94.

19. *Ibid.*, p. 56.

20. Gandhiji has expressed a similar opinion and practised it in his educational experiments ; Harijan, 18-9-1937.

21. Rousseau : *op. cit.*, p. 138.

22. Ross : *op. cit.*, p. 104.

23. It would be profitable to refer to a work by Sir John Adams : 'Modern Developments in Educational Practice', *op. cit.*

24. Ross : *op. cit.*, p. 109.

CHAPTER 4

Idealism in Education

Etimology : There are many misconceptions about the philosophy of idealism, most of which arise from the name itself, which really ought to be 'Idea-ism'. The name 'idealism' arose from 'idea-ism', the 'l' being added for euphony which yields a more pleasing name, one easier to pronounce.[1] Ideaism is the correct usage as the school is distinct for its proclamation that ideas are real.

Exponents : In the western world idealism began with Socrates and Plato. It was Plato who wrote that ideas are real. Since then the world of philosophy has been bedecked with a chain of philosophers who have carried forward and enriched the field. If the world of philosophy is divested of idealistic literature there would hardly remain a body of knowledge which could be pursued as a discipline called philosophy. Some of the linkage names that may be cited are Descartes, Spinoza, Leibniz, Berkeley, Kant, Hegel, Schophenhaur, Fichte, Bergson, Gentile, Bradley, Bosanquet, Emerson, Royce and Horne. Some of these philosophers have expressed their views about education also whereas idealist educational thought has been derived from the philosophic thought of the rest.

MAIN PHILOSOPHICAL IDEAS OF IDEALISM

Idealists hold that mind or spirit as each man experiences it in himself is fundamentally real and that the totality of the universe is spirit in essence. The physical world is just a manifestation of this great spirit behind it. The physical world is destructible and changeable. The idea behind it which is the essence or the spirit of the universe cannot be destroyed. To illustrate the point, one may destroy all the motor cars in the world but the idea of a motor car cannot be destroyed. Ideas are expressions of the mind. The mind is able to create them and they are not perishable. As such the mind is real, whereas matter is subject to decay and destruction. In other words reality is spiritual and not material.

The ultimate reality can be understood and expressed only in terms of ideas. Just as the technological universe is an expression of the ideas of the 'mind' similarly the universe around is an embodiment of the expression of the ideas of the 'Mind'.

Every person has a 'mind' or 'self' or 'spirit' which is spiritual. Individual 'minds' are parts of the universal 'Mind'. As such man is a microcosm within the macrocosm. But all these microcosms cannot by addition make up the macrocosm. The whole has a quality of its own which the parts do not have by themselves. A similar expression in the *Isavasya Upanisad* goes like this :

पूर्णमदं, पूर्णमिदं, पूर्णात पूर्णमुदच्छते ।
पूर्णात पूर्णमादाय, पूर्णमेवा विशिष्यते ॥

Meaning : That (Mind) is a whole and this (individual mind) is a whole, the individual whole is derived from the universal whole (Mind). But even if you subtract the individual whole from the universal whole the latter loses nothing.

To illustrate the above concept with a few concrete examples : White light is made of seven colours. But the white rays have a distinct quality of their own which the seven colours either individually or collectively would not be able to display. Then, the square or for that matter any geometrical figure is made up of lines. The square has a distinct quality of its own which the lines that make it up do not have. The house is something more than the summation of the constituents which go to make it up.

The 'mind' or 'self' which is a part of the 'Mind' manifests itself in and through the body which is matter. Once the individual realises that 'self' then it becomes a part of the 'Self'. There is a very impressive couplet from Kabir that refers to this relationship of the 'self' with the 'Self' :

जल में कुंभ है, कुंभ में जल है ।
फूटा कुंभ, जल, जल ही समान ॥

Another very significant faith that idealists believe in is about the nature of knowledge. For them, knowledge of the heart of spiritual reality (ब्रह्मज्ञान) is the highest and worthiest knowledge. This knowledge can be obtained only through intuition unlike the knowledge of the physical universe which is dependent on the senses. The external world around is a perceived world and not a real world. What is real is the idea behind it. If one does not perceive an object how can one say that it is there. For example, can a person on the outskirts of a forest hear the sound of a falling tree in the heart of the forest. When, as is common knowledge, he is not able to perceive a sound how can he assess that it makes a sound. One can say that it has made a sound only when one has perceived it. Unlike for the normal individuals, for the blind, the world is utter darkness and for the deaf it is an eternal silence. That is why Berkeley had said "*To be, is to be perceived*". As such the external world is only a manifestation of a great reality behind it. The knowledge of this reality which, of course, is possible only through its manifestation is alone real and worthy.

The knowledge of the ultimate reality is not possible through the methods of observation, experimentation, reasoning, etc., which are true guides to the knowledge of the physical universe. Idealists advocate the use of intuition for knowing the ultimate. However, they would use both deductive and inductive logic for understanding the physical universe. The knowledge of the physical universe is basic to the knowledge of the ultimate.

Idealism believes in three spiritual values. They are the Truth, the Beauty and the Goodness. The Truth is an intellectual value, the Beauty an aesthetic value and the Good a moral value. Together they constitute the '*Good*'. For Plato, these three values are identical to each other. As John Keats, the last born and the first to die of the romantic poets, has sung :

'Beauty is Truth and Truth is Beauty
That's all you know on earth and all you need to know '

These values are already there and the purpose of man is to discover them. Man cannot create values. Values are the essences. Essence precedes existence.

IDEALISM IN EDUCATION

Need for Education : Idealists like to educate the child out of two considerations. First of all education is a *spiritual necessity.* It is not just a natural necessity. Nature may give life, but it is education that shows the art of living. Man is born with a biological heritage into a social heritage (culture). It is this culture that he acquires through education that makes a man an individual. Man's nature is spiritual and divine. He can realise this only through education. A natural life will not help in this goal.

Secondly education is also a social necessity. Man is an objective projection of society in an individuated form. Such a projection should reflect *the good* in the society. Hence the need for education and schools. It is common knowledge that ordinarily people of one nation understand form opinions and pass judgements about the quality of social life of another nation through their experiences with the nationals of the respective nation. This is implied in tea-time conversations when observations are made or judgements are passed about the character of people of particular regions also ; for example, Bengalis are like this, Punjabis are like this, Tamilians are like this, etc. As such man may be considered as a projection of a society. Such a projection can appear well through education.

MEANING OF EDUCATION

Education is a process which leads one to the highest moral conduct and deepest spiritual insight. This is an insight into the Truth, the Beauty and the Goodness. Education is a linkage channel between the individual mind and the spiritual environment. It is education that helps an individual to seek the truth and avoid error, enjoy the beauty and discard ugliness, espouse the Good and deprecate evil. As Ross puts it : "The function of education is to help us in our exploration of the ultimate universal values so that the truth of the universe may become our truth and give power to our life."[2]

Man must not submit himself to his natural tendencies and desires. He must be able to suppress them and at times conquer too. For this he needs a strong will power. Immanuel Kant places a lot of premium on the strength and infallibility of the will power in the realisation of the ultimate. Education must be able to develop and fashion this will power in man. The will or the conscience as it is popularly known is inborn. "Education has to feed the conscience by nurturing it in the desired direction."[3]

IDEALISM AND AIMS OF EDUCATION

Idealism forwards two types of aims in education—one for the welfare of the individual and the other for the good of the society. To speak of the former, 'The ultimate aim of education is self-realisation or spiritual becoming.' Self-realisation is the goal of life and hence the aim of education. Such an aim as this is characteristic only of idealism. A self-realised man is an ideal man. He will have internalised the spiritual values. To cite an illustration taking the moral value 'Goodness', a self-realised man does not need to think about his motives and moral consequences of action on others. Virtue will be second-nature with him. He will be virtuous automatically and does not need to try to be so. As Prof. Hiriyanna describes him : "A self-realised man will not be realising virtue but will be revealing it."[4] This is just like observing that the sun reveals light while the earth realises it. The aim of education is to develop the natural man into an ideal man. The ideal man will be possessing physical, intellectual, emotional, moral and spiritual perfection an allround, integrated and complete development.

A self-realised man is a liberated man. Self-realisation means the actualisation of the highest potentialities of the self. Idealists include physical development also as a laudable aim, but they reckon it only as instrumental to the health of the mind or the spirit. They believe that a sound mind can exist only in a sound body. If Naturalism highlights self-expression idealism glorifies self-realisation. Education has to enable the individual to realise all his potential—physical, intellectual, moral and spiritual—in a balanced and integrated way. In brief, education has to fashion a harmoniously integrated personality. Herman H. Horne has given a hierarchy of specific objectives[5] of education in his book Idealism in Education which help to build up an integrated personality.[6]

The social aim of education for the idealists is to have a perfect and genuine democratic society. They prefer a democracy to other forms of society as the values of equality, fraternity, justice and liberty are spiritual in quality. As Horne describes it : "Democracy is a spiritual unity in a social variety."[7] The argument for the establishment of a democracy through education has been concretely stated by Bogoslvsky : "Brotherhood is the soul and essence of real democracy."[8] The idealist aims at realising the brotherhood of men in the democratic society.

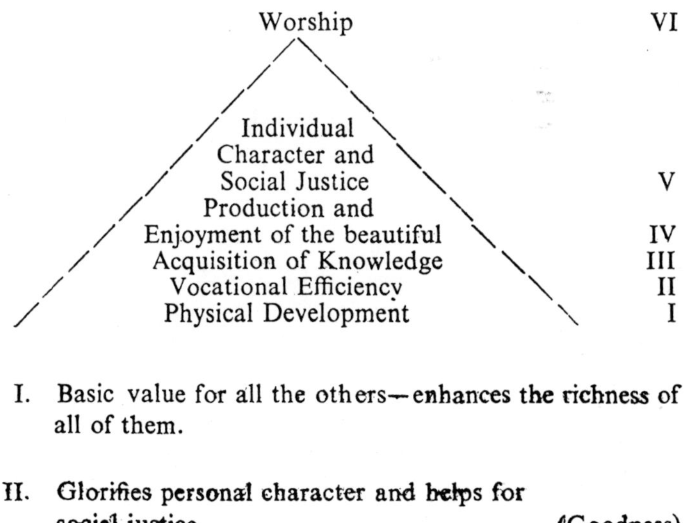

I. Basic value for all the others—enhances the richness of all of them.

II. Glorifies personal character and helps for social justice. (Goodness)

III. Helps to know the nature of the universe. (Truth)

IV. Reveals the perfections in creation. (Beauty)

V. Develops the will of man towards the right. (Goodness)

VI. Brings man into conscious relation with infinite spirit of the universe. (Truth)

However, the individual and social aims of idealist education are complementary to each other. The s nthesis of the two has been impressively expressed by Horne : "Education is the eternal process of superior adjustment of the physically and mentally developed, free, conscious human being to God, as manifested in the intellectual, emotional and volitional environment of man."[9]

IDEALISM AND THE PUPIL

Idealists look at the child as a 'self', a spiritual being. He is also a social being. He is not just an organismic reality but basically a spiritual reality. He is a spiritual unit. He is in the process of becoming. As Horne writes : "Our philosophy dares to suggest that the learner is a finite person, growing, when properly educated, into the image of an infinite person, that his real origin is deity, that his nature is freedom, and that his destiny is immortality."[10] The ultimate reality is a 'being' and the individual is a 'becoming'. The former is Purushothama and the latter is Purusha. The Absolute 'is', the finite 'becomes'. The pupil is in a process of self-actualisation. Education is a necessary condition of the process.

The pupil is also a social being. He can actualise his 'self' only through the service of other 'selves'. Such a belief is the foundation of a modern off-shoot of idealism known as humanistic idealism. Unlike Rousseau who considered the child as good by nature and Hobbes who considered man as base by nature, Idealists look at the child as neither good nor base by nature. They think that he has the potential ('will') either to be good or bad which depends for its actualisation upon the environment and education.

The teacher, and the pupil are equals as both of them are spiritual in nature and have a common goal—'self-realisation'. The teacher because of his age has gone ahead of the pupil towards the goal. He is just like the member of an advance party in a mountaineering expedition.

IDEALISM AND THE CURRICULUM

Idealists like to give to the children such knowledge as is of permanent value. They attach a higher importance to humanities than physical and biological sciences. They would like to teach about culture, art, morality, history, philosophy and literature. They would advocate the teaching of all those subjects that centre around man and aid his moral and spiritual development. They would not object to the teaching of science and technology but are only eager to caution that they must be humanised before they are taught, that is organised and directed towards goals of human welfare. For example, while teaching about the atom it is essential to teach only about its peaceful uses ; teach about the atomic reactor and not the atomic bomb.

A new type of arrangement of the curriculum has been proposed by Bogoslovsky in his work "Ideal School" which is not to be found in the conventional schools. He conceives the curriculum in terms of four inter-related general areas of study directed towards the development of a total personality. They are : the universe division wherein pupils learn about the physical and organismic aspects of the world around them ; the civilisation division which includes the study of social sciences ; the culture division comprising of philosophy, art, religion, etc., and the personality division which touches the physical, physiological, emotional and intellectual aspects of human life. Such an arrangement as this may promote an 'integral view of the universe',[11] as desired by the idealists. But the demarcating lines between different areas will not be distinct.

IDEALISM AND METHODS OF TEACHING

Idealism advocates the use of ideal-centred methods of teaching. That is, while teaching any subject emphasis is placed upon the dignity of man, grandeur and worth of human life and the goals of living. Idealists also believe in self-education of the child, but as distinct from naturalists they would not consider just overt activity as self-activity. Rather they would say that even speculation, meditation and other mental activities also are self-activities. As they would say, appreciation of art is as equally a self-activity as creation of art itself. However, the child must always be conscious of his goals either when he takes to overt activities or keeps to covert activities. As Horne describes self-activity, it is the "power of self-directed pursuit of consciously conceived ends."[12] Idealists value the interests, efforts and most of all the will-power of the child more than their teaching. As the popular saying goes : 'twenty can ride a horse to the pond, but none can make it drink.' According to them, teaching can at best be only a condition of learning and never the cause of it.

For classroom practice, idealists would encourage the use of the discussion and the lecture methods. The discussion method of learning which is popularly known as the Socratic method involves questioning and discussion. It was the method of learning in the Upanisadic period of Indian education. It is also known as the 'informal dialectic' method. Idealists value the use of well-prepared and presented lectures. Lecture should not be a phonographic recitation of facts[13] but a scholarly exposition. It should also not be delivered in an autocratic way. It should be participatory.

Idealism and the School : Idealists attach importance to the school. For them the school is the medium through which the community expresses itself. It is the mind of the society. The very atmosphere of the school should be able to influence the moral and spiritual development of children. For this, the school should build up its own ethos and traditions.

Idealism and Discipline : Idealists like to give 'freedom' to children. But that will be a qualified freedom. It should be for activity. Freedom does not mean licence or waywardness. It implies responsibility. It should be regulated and guided freedom, restrained freedom. Their emphasis is on 'self-discipline'. They believe that human behaviour should have internal controls rather than such external controls as praises and punishments. The place of 'volition' in discipline is highly valued.

Idealism and the Teacher : The position of the teacher in the idealist scheme of education is focal. It is the teacher who provides the key to the educative process. He decides the opportunities for learning and growing for the students and also sets the environment congenial for that. He has to organise the subject-matter and is the mouth piece through which the pupil learns it. He confronts the child as a master of knowledge which the child is going to learn. In no other school of educational philosophy has the teacher such powers as he is bestowed upon by idealism. But idealism equally expects too much from the teacher in terms of his bearing and behaviour. The teacher is reality personified to the child. He must be a specialist in the knowledge of his subject and his pupils. He must be able to command the respect of his pupils by virtue of his scholarship, his teaching, his concern for the students and his overall behaviour, rather than demand it from them. He must awaken in the child the desire to learn. He must be like a personal friend of the student. The teacher is often described as a friend, philosopher and guide. He is described in so many ways as 'a co-worker with God in perfecting man', 'a priest of man's spiritual heritage', 'a perfecter of the mind—the highest form of existence in the cosmos', 'a maker of democracies', 'an apostle of peace and progress' and 'a compendium of all virtues'. However, it is difficult for any teacher to fit into the exacting role—expectations of the idealists.

The teacher is a continuous learner. The adage goes that 'pupils catch fire from a teacher who is himself aflame'. Idealists would approve of Laski's description of a teacher : "He who learns from one who is himself occupied in learning drinks the fresh waters of the running stream. But he who learns from one who has learned all that one is to teach, drinks the green mantle of the stagnant pool."[14]

He must not impose himself on the children and glorify himself. He must try to eliminate himself from the scene as much as possible. He must lose himself in helping the children to grow. The teacher has very well been compared by Froebel to a committed gardener who would see that all his varieties grow to their capacity.

Assessment of Idealism : The contribution of idealism to educational thought is solid and profound. Idealism has provided quite a few lofty aims of education. The aims of education in any educational system have a key role to play as the choice of the matter, method and techniques of evaluation are determined through a chain—process by the aims of education. Idealism as such has influenced educational thought and practice through its aims.

Idealism is a comprehensive philosophy. It has something to say about all aspects of educational theory and practice. In doing so at every stage it highlights the human and personal elements in life and education.

There are numerous criticisms to the idealistic tradition of philosophy from various quarters. In fact, some of the other schools of thought owe their origin and development to idealism as they grew out of a protest, reaction or a revolt against this school. However, the mere number of criticisms against the school do not detract anything from the values of idealism as a distinct contributor to educational thought.

One of the criticisms against Idealism refers to its abstractness. It has been described as an abstract philosophy and a visionary utopia. It hijacks one from immediate realities as it is biased towards ultimate realities. Another significant criticism though not fully justifiable, is that it under-rates the study of science and technology and is inimical to experimental methods of learning. It is also criticised for supporting the over-dependence of the learner on the teacher.

REFERENCES

1. Ivor Morrish : "Disciplines of Education", Allen & Unwin, London, 1967, p. 35.
2. Ross : "Groundwork of Educational Theory", p. 123.
3. Butler : *op. cit.*, p. 213.
4. Hiriyanna : "Outlines of Indian Philosophy", Allen and Unwin, London, 1932, p. 381.
5. Refer to p. 64 of the book.
6. Horne, H. H. : "Idealism in Education".
7. Horne, H. H. : "The New Education", Abingden Press, New York, 1931, p. 118.
8. Bogoslovsky : "The Ideal School", Macmillan Co., New York, 1936, p. 520.
9. Horne : "The Philosophy of Education", p. 285.
10. "An Idealistic Philosophy of Education", in 42nd year book of the NSSE, Part I, Public School Pub. Co., Bloomington Ill., 1942, p, 155.

11. Dr. Radhakrishnan has defined the aim of university education as an attempt to "give an integrated picture of the universe"—University Education Commission Report, 1948.

12. Horne, H. H. : 'The Philosophy of Education', Macmillan Co., N.Y., 1937, pp. 170-171.

13. There is a funny definition of lecture which fits into many of the lectures delivered by some of the teachers. "It is a mysterious process wherein words travel from the handbook of the teacher to the notebook of the students without passing through the mind of either."

14. Quoted after S.R. Dongerkerry, "British Universities".

CHAPTER 5

Pragmatism

Etymology : The term pragmatism is derived from the Greek word 'pragma' which means action, from which words like 'practice' and 'practical' have been derived. Charles Peirce introduced this word into philosophy. It suggests an emphasis upon the practicalities of life and that the practicable is the real.

What is Pragmatism ? : It will be useful to know the contexts in which this word was used by William James who can be taken to be one of the earliest exponents of the school. In his book 'Pragmatism', James described it thus: "The pragmatic method is primarily a method of solving metaphysical disputes which are unending."[1] For example, there are a number of problems in philosophy for which there are controversial solutions. 'Is the world one or many', 'fated or free', 'material or spiritual' are only a few illustrations. Pragmatism offers to solve these problems by suggesting that one must trace the practical consequences of either of the solutions. In a way it does not attach much importance to the age-long metaphysical problems of philosophy. As William James exemplifies the point : "A pragmatist turns his back resolutely and once for all upon a lot of inveterate habits dear to professional philosophers. He turns away from abstraction and insufficiency, from verbal solutions, from bad *a priori* reason, from fixed principles, closed systems, and pretended absolutes and origins. He turns towards concreteness and adequacy, towards facts, towards action, and towards power."[2] It is clear from the above assertion that pragmatism is a method wherein one looks away from first principles and looks towards last things or consequences of action. It is basically an attitude or a frame of mind and not a body of ideas. It welcomes any idea which is testable and which leads to favourable consequences. As the Italian pragmatist Papini would claim : "It lies in the midst of our theories like a corridor in a hotel, innumerable chambers open out of it. In one you may find a man writing an atheistic volume ; in the next some-one on his knees praying for faith and strength ; in a third a chemist investigating the properties of a body ; in a fourth a system of idealist metaphysics is excogitated ; in a fifth the impossibility of metaphysics is being shown. But they all own the corridor and all must pass through it if they want a practicable way of getting into or out of their respective rooms."[3] Pragmatism is herein conceived of as a testing ground of all ideas. It does not give ideas, but it verifies them. If Idealism speaks of ideas and ideals, pragmatism is concerned only with facts. Other equivalent names for pragmatism are 'Instrumentalism' and 'Experimentalism'. Any idea which is instrumental to success, which works, is real or true ; hence, 'instrumentalism'.

Representatives : The roots of pragmatism can be traced back to ancient Greek philosophy. Heraclitus and the Sophists of ancient Greece are considered to be pragmatic in their approach to life. There were other contemporaries such as Protagoras and Gorgias. In the sixteenth century Francis Bacon (1561-1626) preferred and advocated the empirical approach to the rational approach which is the basis of pragmatic method. In recent times, Charles S. Pierce, William James, John Dewey, W.H. Kilpatrick, J.L. Childs and Ratner are the representative writers in the field. Of all of them, John Dewey has been able to influence educational practice of the United States in particular and the world at large. He even visited China in the early part of this century and left an impact on their educational thinking.

MAIN PHILOSOPHICAL IDEAS OF PRAGMATISM

It is rather difficult to present a list of philosophical ideas of pragmatism as pragmatists do not believe in speculations. To quote Dewey : "The chief characteristic of the pragmatic notion of reality is precisely that no theory of reality in general is possible or needed."[4] The belief is more clearly expressed by Judges : "Your energies are misdirected if you worry about cosmic purpose or divine truths, or lie awake in the night perplexed by intellectual difficulties and terrors of limitless time and ever extending space."[5] In fact, one of the criticisms against pragmatism, as will be referred to at the end of the discussions about the school, is that it is metaphysically insufficient. However, the later exponents of the field have been able to derive and consolidate the views of pragmatism about the problems of philosophy. Such an attempt has been well made by Dr. J.L. Childs.[6] They are presented as follows :

The observations of pragmatism centre around the world[7] of human experience. It is not concerned with the discovery of some all-embracing invisible reality that gives a meaning to human experiences and actions. The world is all foreground for them. It is not, nor does it include a 'trans-empirical' reality (contrast it with the 'supernatural' of Naturalism). As such they believe in the non-theistic, non-mystical, non-spiritual (it is everywhere 'non' not 'anti') character of existence.

Pragmatists believe that reality (world) is in a constant flux. The world is in a state of continuous change. It is a process. It is just like the ever-changing waters of an on-going stream. There is nothing in the world which is static, permanent or eternal. Everything is in flux and movement. Heraclitus is attributed to have said, "One cannot step twice into the same river." There is a good coverage of 'Change in Modern Life' in one of Kilpatrick's works.[8] There is change in the physical, social, political, economic and such other institutional organisations and environments of man.

As the world is subject to change and as change means unpredictability and probabilities of danger, there is not complete security in it. One must be prepared for the worst though hoping for the best. One of the chapters in Dewey's 'Experience and Nature'[9] refers to this aspect. One cannot be conclusive about the goodness or evil of the world. As such, the pragmatist would neither support optimism nor appreciate pessimism. He would only exhort human beings to put in their utmost effort to improve the human situation but does not assure the final end. He believes that the world does not guarantee progress. He assumes the golden path, the middle-of-the-road position in the age old disagreements between exponents of free-will and determinism. The pragmatist firmly believes that human effort will improve the human situation. The world for him is incomplete and indeterminate. It is unfinished and still growing. As such there is scope to improve. As James had said, 'the past was not perfect, the present is not satisfactory, the future is partially controllable.'

Man is not different from reality. He is a part of the world and continuous with it. Though he is a knowing creature, he is not different from the known. The theory of evolution bears testimony to this belief.

Knowledge based on common experience is true, genuine and worthy of acquisition. Pragmatists give secondary importance to reading and speculation. They do not give credence to intuitive knowledge. Knowledge gained through doing, acting and living is useful. That knowledge which is helpful in solving present day problems is most preferred. In a way, they emphasise functional knowledge and understanding. Even with respect to ideas they would say that those which influence practice are real. The meaning of an idea is its influence on practice. Truth or falsity of an idea depends on its practice. Truth of an idea means its power to work. If ideas work, they are true. If idealists say 'ideas are real', pragmatists would say 'ideas become real'. Truth happens to an idea. One must experiment an idea and the result he gets therein would be instrumental in determining the truth of the idea. It is because of this belief that pragmatism is also referred to as instrumentalism and experimentalism. They emphasise that always tested practices must be adopted.

They believe in the use of reason only in indeterminate situations. They are also referred to as crossroad or forked or problematic situations. These are situations which are disturbing, ambiguous, troubling, confusing, puzzling, obscure and full of conflicting tendencies, but not causing panic. However, the end of reason and logic is action. They do not approve of reasoning for its own sake.

Pragmatism does not believe in standard, permanent, eternal values. For them values emerge only in individual—social flow of events. Values are obtained from society. If there is no society, no organisation, however small it is, for an individual who lives in utter isolation where is the question of being honest, responsible, sincere, loyal or outspoken. All morality is social in essence. Values are changing. They are also in a state of flux. They vary spatially and temporally. The validity of a value has to be determined from the consequences of putting it into action.

PRAGMATISM IN EDUCATION

Need for Education : Education is necessary for an individual because of two reasons. It is on one hand a natural and on the other a social necessity. Education is a natural necessity because, unlike the off-springs of other living creatures, human off-springs depend for over a decade on adults for their physiological development. However, education is basically a social necessity. It is a social function. It is through education that an individual is socialised and the society gets renewal. Education is necessary for the stability and continuity of all societies. But such a need is pronounced in a democratic society. As Dewey has pointed out : "A Government resting upon popular suffrage cannot be successful unless those who elect and obey their governors are educated."[10]

Meaning of Education : Natural tendencies of an individual do not conform to the life-customs of the group. Education is direction of these natural tendencies to make them conform likewise. The result of direction is growth. Growth is a characteristic of life. As education is growth and as growth is a characteristic of life, education is life itself.[11]

Education is also a social function. The school is a special environment which carries out this function. The school is in fact a social invention that serves a social need. Education does not mean teaching the child as is done in conventional schools. It is rather encouraging the child to learn for himself through experimental activities, participation, direct experiencing and through 'doing'.

Aims of Education : Pragmatism does not believe in setting general aims of education. The general aim of education is more education. There can only be specific objectives to each learning situation. General objectives will fit into a set way of life and do not enable the child to adjust himself to the demands of changing life. They do not develop an experimental frame of mind. As Ross describes : "Since life itself is experimental there is no definite goal towards which the child must advance. Any attempt on the part of the educator to prescribe goals or to decide the child's purposes for himself stultifies true education."[12] As such the pupil must be given such experiences as would help him to make the most of subsequent experiences. Education must develop the power of effective experiencing. The pupil must be enabled to cope with the indeterminancies of life. Even the specific objectives must be focused, clear, concrete, practicable and oriented towards human welfare. "Pragmatism stresses human purposes and satisfaction of human wants rather than one grand purpose towards which the universe is to move."[13] This is a reflection against the 'ideal man' and 'ideal society', of Idealism.

However, a few aims of education could be identified, which are general in nature, in the writings of pragmatists.[14] Natural development and social efficiency are the two aims of education, conceived by Dewey. Natural development refers to the development of bodily organs and the maintenance of health and vigour. It also includes the development of physical skills that would be useful in games and plays and in handling materials. Educators should recognise the individual differences in the natural development of children.

Social efficiency is another aim of education. Natural urges do not agree with the life-customs of the group. The function of education is to habituate an individual to social control, to develop a willingness to subordinate his natural urges to social rules. Social efficiency includes industrial competence and good citizenship. Industrial competence refers to economic efficiency and economic control or value of thrift. Good citizenship means the ability to judge men and measures wisely and to take a determining part in making as well as obeying laws. It means a capacity to share in a give and take of experience. Such a capacity is essential especially in a democratic system of education as democracy means shared power and shared responsibility.

Pragmatism and the Pupil : The child is creative and constructive by nature. He is not a passive listener but an active participant in the educative process. Educators must exploit the activities of children for the teaching-learning process.

The child is also a social being. Unlike the previous conception of education as a bipolar process, the child and the educative process being the two poles, pragmatists think of it as a tri-polar process, the immediate society being the third pole. The child needs to be familiarised with the life-customs, traditions, folkways, mores, norms, values and behaviour-patterns of the society, or, rather socialised.

PRAGMATISM AND THE CURRICULUM

Pragmatists neither approve of a rigid, traditional pattern of curriculum wherein there would be water-tight compartmentalisation of knowledge into different subjects nor do they support a *laissez-faire* policy in curriculum organisation. They believe in a certain degree of organisation of the curriculum. They would also like to integrate the curriculum with the life and experiences of children. To quote Dewey : "The child and the curriculum are simply two limits which define a single process."[15] Pragmatists prefer to give integrated knowledge around particular and significant problems of life rather than divide knowledge into various subjects of instruction. A study of social, economic and political institutions, current social, economic and political problems, natural resources and such other similar studies can form the curriculum. School studies should be integrated as their counterparts in the world are integrated. Life and experience of the pupil should be integrated with the activities of the school.

PRAGMATISM AND METHODS OF TEACHING

The focus of pragmatic methods of teaching is on the 'child-in-society' and his activities therein rather than the book, the teacher, the subject or exclusively the child-of-nature. Learning always occurs as a result of movement and activity. The teacher has to capitalise upon the activities of children to direct the teaching-learning process. Activity is the basis of all teaching. The child should be enabled to find out information by himself instead of pouring information on him. Children should be encouraged to discover and investigate the facts of life. Education must develop the 'laboratory habit of mind'. The method of teaching should be experimental.

Dewey feels that methods of teaching should develop reflective thinking in children. They must ask the 'why ?' of things and not merely the 'how ?' of things. Method cannot be conceived in isolation from matter. Therefore, method should vary as matter varies.

To speak of the actual methods employed in classrooms, pragmatists lean on creative and constructive projects. Project is a purposive activity rooted in real life. As W.H. Kilpatrick has defined it : "A project is a whole-hearted purposeful activity proceeding in a social environment." Only problems that appeal to common-sense are posed. As J.A. Stevenson has defined it : "An educational project is a problematic act carried to its completion in its natural setting."[16] Artificial problems have no place in projects. As education is life itself and as artificiality has no place in life, projects need to centre around real problems. As P.B. Ballard has defined it : "A project is a bit of real life that has been imparted into the school." Projects may be workedout outside the school also. They take note of the constructive efforts of children. Experience is the main objective to be realised. Knowledge is only a by-product and incidental to the activity.

There are four stages in the project method. They are : purposing, planning, executing and evaluating. Students participate at all the four stages. Projects may be worked by any individual or a group. In either case these steps have to be followed. However, pragmatists would prefer group projects as they allow for co-operation, participation in group-life and and sharing of responsibilities.

Preparing common salt, dissecting a frog, making an electric bell, digging a well, make-believe post offices, banks, shops, farms and mock parliaments are only a few illustrations which allow for project work. For example, while digging a well children learn about the sources, composition and properties of water and also conduct a few experiments on water.

Pragmatism also encourages discussion as a method of learning. Discussion is a form of group-thinking and is a method of learning in the community. It also encourages laboratory work, personal reference in the library, educational tours and excursions.

Pragmatism and the School : A school need not imply a number of classrooms wherein benches are systematically arranged in parallel rows on which pupils have to sit and listen continuously to the expositions of teachers one after the other on different subjects throughout the day. Even a workshop and a laboratory can be a school for them. In fact, any social environment which inspires the children for experimentation constitutes a school for them.

School is the embryo of the community.[17] It has to provide an embryonic community life for children. For this it has to organise itself on a social basis. The school is an instrument of transmission and transformation of the culture of the group. It can perform this function in three ways—

(*a*) *Simplification and Organisation* : Society has a complex organisation. The school is to be society in miniature and it can be a simple and well-knit society.

(*b*) *Purification and Selection* : The school should represent only the good and the desirable in society.

(*c*) *Genuine Representation* : It should not be an agent of some segment of society, may be a political or a religious group. It should not provide a limited cultural perspective.

PRAGMATISM AND DISCIPLINE

Pragmatists would like to give a lot of freedom to children. They are only anxious that it should not be mistaken for licence. The teacher, in the capacity of adviser and guide, and the pursuit of the self-activity of the child should together promote self-discipline. They do not believe in the old adage, 'Work while you work and play while you play'. Rather they advocate a discipline that can be maintained through play as work.[18] Work can become play if it is rooted in the interest of the child. For example, cricket becomes work if it is played out of coercion and a mathematical riddle becomes play if it is solved out of zeal. Dewey believes that discipline is closely associated with interest. If the activities of children are rooted in the interests, specific needs, capabilities and preferences of children then there is no problem of discipline. As such the interests of the child should be aroused, sustained and satisfied.

PRAGMATISM AND THE TEACHER

The teacher is not a dictator but only 'a leader of group activities'. He should not overshadow the personality of the pupil. He has to plan and organise the teaching-learning situation, provide learning experiences and opportunities for experimentation. He must not impose himself on children. The teacher should treat the pupils as his own equals in regard to social life.

ASSESSMENT OF PRAGMATISM

The significant contribution of pragmatism to educational practice is that it has been able to infuse realism into it, a perception of the practicalities of life and a respectful attitude towards the solution of day-to-day problems of living. It keeps the children close to their experiences and exhorts the educational system to capitalise upon that. It has promoted the values of experimentation in educational practice. The 'project method' of learning and the associated values of democratic beliefs and actions is the single most important contribution of pragmatism to educational practice.

However, one of the criticisms that is often made against pragmatism is that it does not encourage the development of individuality in children owing to its view of children as exclusively social beings. Also, pragmatism has not been able to solve the riddle of the universe—its origin, nature, purpose and destiny. Instead of explaining, it has explained away the universe. In this sense, it is metaphysically insufficient. About the project method it is felt that, through it, organisation of knowledge would be difficult. It can only be used in limited ways but not as a method of school education for all subjects and topics.

REFERENCES

1. W. James "Pragmatism", Longmans, Greens and Co., N.Y., 1914, p. 45.
2. *Ibid.*
3. *Ibid.*, p. 54, Quoted after William James, Longmans, Greens and Co., New York, 1914.
4. "Creative Intelligence" Holt, Rinehart & Winston, New York, 1917, p. 55.

5. "Education and the Philosophic Mind", p. 83.
6. "Education and the Philosophy of Experimentalism" Ch. III, "Has Experimentalism a Metaphysic ?" Appleton Century, N.Y., 1931.
7. 'World' is synonymous with the words Cosmos, Nature and Reality.
8. 'Philosophy of Education', Chapter V, Macmillan, New York, 1963.
9. Chapter II, 'Existence as precarious and as stable.'
10. "Democracy and Education", *op. cit.*, p. 87.
11. For a fuller discussion of the meaning of education the reader may refer to pages of the book. Chapter II, Dewey : "Democracy and Education".
12. 'Groundwork of Educational Theory', *op. cit.*, p. 138.
13. Ross : "Groundwork of Educational Theory", p. 139.
14. Dewey : 'Democracy and Education', Chapters VIII and IX.
15. "Child and the Curriculum", University of Chicago Press, Chicago, Phoenix Books, 1956, p. 11.
16. 'The Project Method of Teaching', p. 43.
17. Dewey : "School and Society", University of Chicago Press, Chicago, Phoenix Books, 1956, p. 18.
18. Dewey : 'Democracy and Education', Chapter X.

CHAPTER 6

Realism in Education

Etimology

Realism emerged as a movement in philosophy against the extreme idealist view of the world around. Idealists are well known for their belief in the temporality of the world and their faith in the essence behind it. But some of them went far beyond to disbelieve in the existence of the world itself. Berkeley who may be taken to represent the position proclaimed the now famous "To be, is to be perceived". The external world depends on the perceptions of individuals and as such is a subjective reality. However, a number of criticisms were forged against this view both from idealist and other quarters. John Locke and his contemporaries affirmed that the world around is a real world and not a world of fantasy. It is not based on perceptions but is an objective reality. Hence the name realism.

Exponents

The realist trend in philosophy can be traced back to Aristotle who interested himself in particular facts of life as against Plato who was interested in abstractions and generalities. Another great name of the school is Saint Thomas Aquinas who infused the realist spirit in religion. Comenius, in his 'Great Didactic' wrote that mind is only a passive recipient reflecting all things around it as a spherical mirror. John Locke put it more vehemently when he said that "the mind is a 'tabula rasa' (clean slate) and reality is outside the mind." After him philosophers and thinkers like Immanuel Kant, John Freiderich Herbart and William James affirmed that the external world is a real world.

Realist movement was received vigorously in the twentieth century when six American Professors led by Barton Perry published a book in 1912 titled as "The New Realism". Another group was formed in 1916 who styled themselves as critical realists and published a book in 1920 titled as "Essays in Critical Realism." Arthur Lovejoy, Johns Hopkins and George Santayana belonged to this group.[1]

Main Philosophical Ideas of Realism

The world around is a reality. It is a world of objects and not ideas. It is a pluralistic world—a world of materials, a world of ideas and a world of experiences. The world is a mechanism. There is a order and design in the world. Man is a part of this order. The world is self-caused and ruled by the laws of cause and effect relationships. As such there is no freedom of the will for man. The mind of man is only a brain-function. As such mind is also matter. There have been quite a few experiments in recent times using electronic devices and controlling certain parts of the brain. During such controls it was observed that the organism lost the associated mental powers such as memory and thinking.

As reality is outside the mind and as the world around is an objective reality, knowledge of the surrounding world is the most desirable knowledge. The best method to acquire knowledge is the experimental or the scientific method. Alfred North Whitehead and Bertrand Russel advocate the exclusive use of this method. One has to define the problem to be solved, observe all the facts relating to the problem, formulate a hypothesis, test it and accept the verified solution.

Realists do not believe in ideal values. They would like to discover values in the immediate social life. The external world consisting of men and matter would provide the framework for value-discovery and value-realisation.

REALISM IN EDUCATION

Need for Education : Education is a cultural necessity. Man is born with a biological heritage into a social heritage. It is necessary to transform the biological organism into a cultured gentleman. John Locke has dwelt in detail about the education of a 'gentleman' in his work 'On Education'.

Meaning of Education : Education for the realist is a preparation for life. The young child when grown up has to perform many roles such as that of a citizen, a worker, a husband or a housewife, a member of a group, etc. To fit into these roles effectively the child needs education. In this sense education is a preparation for life.

Aims of Education : Realists do not believe in general or 'Common aims' of education. Aims are specific to each individual and his perspectives. The pupil, teacher, parent, administrator, political leader, etc., have different perspectives.

As such how can there be a general aim suited to all persons. However, if one insists that realists must come out with such a general aim then Dr. Broudy presents such an overall aim of education. Dr. Broudy who presents the realist view point in education defines the common aim of education as a preparation for the "*Good Life*". As Broudy defines it in the context of the school : "The task of the school is to transcribe the good life, the good individual and the good society into learnings that presumably will contribute to their production."[2] The basic questions remains as to what constitutes a 'good life' and how to realise it. In answer, Dr. Broudy would suggest one must study human nature and understand the dynamics of a healthy personality. A healthy personality who can be supposed to be capable of leading a good life is governed by four principles. They are the principles of self-preservation, self-determination, self-realisation and self-integration. Self-preservation is an appetitive principle and is the physiological base of a healthy personality. 'Self-determination' guides the person to visualise reality and understand his strengths and limitations. The individual would develop a 'free-will' based on his reality-perception. Free-will does not mean the ability to do whatever one desires. It is the means to carry-out well thoughtout decisions ; it is the willingness to work hard, to avoid routine and to plan one's actions. Self-realisation as it is used by realists has a different meaning than the one implied by idealists. Here it means that every individual will have certain congenital potentialities and there are also differences in the degree and breadth of such potentialities from person to person. The realisation of these potentialities by a person is called as self-realisation. It is not transcendental perfection. It is individualistic and social at the same time. Education must enable a person to actualise his potentialities. Self-integration refers to the integrated development of an individual.

To state the aims of education in a concrete way and make it intelligible, acquisition of knowledge is an important objective of education. Other objectives include the development of character and vocational efficiency.

Realism and the Pupil : The pupil is an organism with a highly developed brain. He has the ability to read meaning into his experiences, conceive purposes and work to realise them. Pupil must be given freedom to decide about his activities and in executing them. Then alone the child can get reality-orientation in life.

Realism and the Curriculum : Curriculum for the realists is a means of forming desirable habits. These habits are to be acquired not through conditioning but through the mastery of subject-matter. As Dr. Broudy writes : "The objectives of the curriculum are to develop habits and skills of acquiring, using and enjoying truth. It is suggested that the way to form these habits is by mastery of organised subject-matter."[3] Mastery of the subject-matter does not mean memorisation of facts. It is rather the understanding and application of knowlege in planning, deciding and executing actions. Realists prefer a system of general education over a period of time at the earlier stages and specialisation to come later. At later stages they would like to give a vocational bias to the curriculum. Subjects of the curriculum would include courses in physics, chemistry, mathematics, life sciences and their application, social sciences in an integrated way and self-sciences such as literature, biography, philosophy, psychology and art. They do not advocate a separate curriculum for moral education.

Realism and Methods of Teaching : Realists would encourage the use of lectures, discussions and symposia. They believe in the Socratic method of learning. They would not object to memorisation at the earlier stages. They advocate the profuse employment of audio-visual methods in teaching. Audio-visual aids enable the teacher to develop sensory powers in children. Children would have clearer 'feel' of reality through them. They believe that the place of motivation is very important in the teaching-learning situation. Realists value insight-learning as of a superior quality.

Realism and the Teacher : The teacher in a realist-school must be a scholar. Though they want men of high character and integrity still they believe that they would be of no avail to children unless coupled with mastery of information. The teacher is only a guide to children. He must neither be a pessimist nor an optimist but guide the children towards the hard realities of life. He must expose children to the problems of life and the world around.

Assessment of Realism : Realism is a practical philosophy and it preaches one to come to terms with reality. Its emphasis on reality-orientation would help an individual to preserve his mental health. In a vast expanding scientific and technological universe where knowledge increases exponentially, a philosophy that justifies the acquisition of knowledge is worth its place.

Realism is often criticised for its 'undue' emphasis on knowledge and neglect of the child. The modern trend in educational thought being paido-centric, Realism is said to have put the clock behind the times by placing its highest priority on knowledge.

REFERENCES

1. Joseph L. Blau : "Men and Movements in American Philosophy", Prentice-Hall Inc., New York, 1953, Chapter 8, pp. 274-312.
2. "Building a Philosophy of Education", Prentice-Hall, New Delhi, 1965, p. 25.
3. *Op. cit.*, p. 309.

CHAPTER 7

Existentialism and Education

Introductory Remarks

A keen study of quite an amount of existentialist philosophy would reveal that to write about existentialism is neither easy nor simple but a challenging and complex one, not because it requires any special talent to either understand or explain it but because of the inherent paradoxes and ambiguities in the philosophy itself. It is difficult to be fully intelligible and coherent when one writes about existentialism. If doubts and confusions are left uncleared, one can only say that 'contradictions and inconsistencies are fundamental to their thought.'[1] Some illustrations of such paradoxes are—Heidegger's statement : 'analyse death to understand life', Jaspers : 'Renounce your world and you will return to it', Sartre : 'You are a free man if you deny God', Kierkegaard : 'You are a free man if you accept God', etc. When once a critique drew the attention of Sartre by his remark : 'Your philosophy is problematic and ambiguous', Sartre's reply was 'Man does seem to me to be ambiguous.'[2] Not only their thought, even their language is obscure. Here is an example of existentialist dialectical confusion : 'Nothing' is revealed in dread, but not as something that 'is'. Neither can it be taken as an object. Dread is not an apprehension of Nothing. All the same, nothing is revealed in and through dread, yet not, again, in the sense that Nothing appears as if detached and apart from what-is-in-totality when we have that 'uncanny' feeling. We would say rather : in dread Nothing functions as if *at one with* WHAT-IS-IN-TOTALITY.[3] Another very significant source of confusion arises out of the differing personal lives and convictions of existential philosophers. For example, Kierkegaard, Marcel and Jaspers are theists whereas Sartre and Heidegger are agnostics. Jaspers is a protestant whereas Marcel is a staunch Roman Catholic. Less said the better about the diversities of other existentialist philosophers like Berdyaev, Buber, Tillich and Neibhur.

In my opinion, the mark of a good writing is that it must satisfy three conditions. It must be cojent, coherent and consistent. I am afraid that I might not present to you a coherent view of existentialism though I can attempt to realise the other two as, existentialists themselves believe that a theory need not be coherent still contain the truth within it.

Historical Overview

Just as the whole of Indian philosophy is either an extension, interpretation, criticism and corroboration of the Vedas and in it the Upanisads or an outright revolt against them, similarly it may be remarked of Western philosophy as either a clarification of Socrates or his rejection. One would be still right in saying that the whole of Western Philosophy is an appendix on

Socrates. So it is even true with existentialism that Socrates has been considered[4] to be the first existentialist because of his statement : "I am and always have been a man to obey nothing in my nature except the reasoning which, upon reflection, appears to me to be the best." We will be correct in this assertion only when we think of Socratic method as existentialistic rather than Socratic thought because existentialism is a negation of Socratic philosophy itself. Right from Plato down to (Spinoza, Leibnitz) Descartes, the majority of western thinkers have been believing in the immutability of ideas and the rest of the thinkers have been suggesting, correctives to it. Anyhow their frame of reference has always been *Essence Precedes Existence*, essence being referred to ideas, values, ideals, thoughts, etc., and existence being referred to our lives. The last in the series was Hegel who carried farthest this effort to understand the world rationally.

But by the middle of the 19th Century there sprang up a Danish philosopher, Soren Kierkegaard (1813-1855) who not only rejected the Platonic view but reversed the order itself. Kierkegaard, who may be considered to be the founder of the philosophy of existence contradicted Hegel and asserted that *Existence Precedes Essence.* Kierkegaard revolted against not any one school of philosophy in particular but the whole of philosophy itself. It was a revolt against the whole method of philosophy itself, which has been supported by all the other existentialists. The existential method is an individualistic method. Existentialists are against any kind of rationalisations, universalities and generalities in philosophy. They have advocated extreme subjectivism in philosophising. As Marcel claims himself to be : "I have played the part of a prosecuting attorney against every philosophy that seemed to me to remain the prisoner of abstractions."[5]

Kierkegaard's life and works were not of any significance for his contemporaries[6] and it took nearly a century for a revival of his thinking, when there was a translation of his major work 'Either/or' (The problem of life for Kierkegaard was always an either/or, the proverbial to be, or not to be of Shakespeare's *Hamlet*) in English and German.

At least for the Western world, the first half of the twentieth century has been an age marked by anxieties, conflicts, sufferings, tragic episodes, dread, horror, anguish, persecution and human sacrifices caused mainly by the two intermittent world wars. Here was an occasion for philosophising. As Harper writes : "Tragedy, death, guilt, suffering all force one to appraise one's total situation, much more than do happiness, joy, success, innocence, since it is in the former that momentous choices must be made."[7] So. there sprang up a group of philosophers spread all over Germany, France and Italy which were the places of social crisis. Significant among these philosophers were Karl Jaspers and Martin Heidegger[8] from Germany. Karl Jaspers was Professor of Philosophy at Heidelberg and Heidegger was Professor of Philosophy at Freiburg. France contributed two other existentialists for the world of philosophy; one of them was Gabriel Marcel a philosopher and playwright and another Jean Paul Sartre, a great litterateur and philosopher (Professor of philosophy at Sorborne). There are quite a few gentlemen who are associated remotely with the philosophy of existentialism like Schelling, Nietsche, Pascal, Hussrell who have influenced existential thought but cannot be rigidly classified as existentialists. Existentialism thus has a short history of nearly two centuries.

Philosophy of Existentialism

Author has rather hesitant to discuss existentialism as a school of Philosophy as author would easily discuss idealism, pragmatism, utilitarianism or other schools of philosophy, because existentialists themselves do not like it. Heidegger was angry at being called as an existentialist. In fact, the whole of the philosophy is a revolt against system-building (in contrast to Plato, Descartes, Spinoza, Leibniz and Kant) in philosophy and the consequent mechanisation, abstraction and rationalisation of human existence. Therefore, instead of discussing existentialism systematically in terms of metaphysics, epistemology, axiology, logic, etc. I prefer to discuss some of the existential concepts which I may use later to derive implications for education.

At the outset, let us discuss their concept of philosophy. Philosophy is an interpretation of our inner life—of our experiences, and our experiences are so unique[9] and subjective that there is neither scope nor sense in generalisations about human experience. Philosophy is not a search for truth but a trial of truth. They say that it is not enough if you 'know' the truth, you must 'exist' the truth, because life is not a riddle to be solved but a reality to be experienced. Philosophy must grow out of your reflections over your experiences of life and not grow out of wonder (Thales), or love of truth or your keen interest in human life. As Allen puts it : "It is an attempt at philosophising from the standpoint of the actor instead of, as has been customary from that of the spectator."[10] With this conception of philosophy, it can be convincingly argued that the whole of classical Indian philosophy is existential in nature. As Prof. Hiriyanna has said, philosophy in India has been the fruit of speculations of sages over the practical problems of life that they encountered.[11(a)(b)] Even Dr. Radhakrishnan[11(c)] affirms that "Every major system of Indian philosophy takes its beginning from the practical and tragic problems of life and searches for the truth in order to solve the problem of man's distress in the world in which he finds himself. It is said that existentialism is a philosophy of crisis. A crisis in an individuals' or group life is an occasion for philosophy. In this sense, the whole of Bhagavad Gita can be considered as an existential treatise as "The teaching of the Gita must not be regarded in the light of a general spiritual philosophy or ethical doctrine, but as bearing upon a practical crisis in the application of ethics and spirituality to human life."[12] The occasion for philosophising has been the situation in which Arjuna is placed—the proverbial 'to be, or not to be', Kierkegaard's

"Either/or", 'to fight or not to fight', as Arjuna asks Krishna :

अपि त्रैलोक्यराज्यस्य हेतोः किं नु महीकृते

(When I do not kill them for the sovereignty of the three world's, why should I for this earth).[13]

A number of similar occasions of existential choice as can be identified in the epics and upanisads of India like Rama's decision to send Sita to the forest, Nachiketa's decision to refuse the pleasures of life (Katha Upanisad), Siddhartha's decision to become Buddha are all occasions for philosophising. As such it can be easily shown that "both existentialism and classical Indian philosophy agree that what occasions philosophical enquiry is not mere intellectual curiosity but a crisis in the individual's life, which calls upon him to make a 'choice' regarding his subsequent existence."[14] In fact the very etymological meaning of 'existence' from two German words 'ex-sistet'[15] meaning that which stands out, that which 'emerges' suggests that existentialism is a philosophy that emerges out of problems of life. In brief, as Marcel conceives of it philosophy is a counsellor in crisis.

Basic Concepts of Existentialism

One of the fundamental, foundational concepts of existentialism is that "Existence precedes essence." It was Plato who said that the surrounding world is a world of essences—ideas, and the purpose of life is to discover these essences. Essences are already there and they precede existence. Even existence is an embodiment of an essence—the self, which is a part of an universal essence—the Self. The majority of other western philosophers carried forward this theory. Descartes even affirmed the reality of existence becaure of its essence—thinking, as he said 'I think, therefore, I am'. Bergson even went to the extreme of saying that 'I do not think, it (essence) thinks in me', thereby striking a transcendental, desperately deterministic note on human existence. Similarly naturalist philosophers rejected this type of a transcendental determinism but replaced it by a naturalistic determinism by identifying essences in nature as preceding existence. On the other hand pragmatists spoke of social determinism. As such, existentialism is a revolt against any kind of determinism and an affirmation of the free nature of man. They not only affirm that existence is prior to essence, that man is fundamentally free to create his essences, but think that this is the tragedy about man. Man is not only free, but ironically he is condemned to be free. Sartre's monumental work "Being and Nothingness"[16] is basically a formulation of this theory of man. As Blackham writes : "But for Sartre, there is no creator of man. Man discovered himself. His existence came first; he now is in the process of determining his essence. Man first *is*, then he defines himself."[17] Therefore, man is conceived of as a free, responsible, aspiring and striving becoming[18] instead of as a helpless, despondent being—a creature waiting to realise what is given to him. As Sartre himself explains this concept to us, "What is meant here by saying that 'existence precedes essence.' " It means that, first of all, man exists, turns up, appears on the scene, and, only afterwards defines himself. If man, as the existentialist sees him is indefinable, it is because at first he is nothing. Only afterwards will he be something and *he himself will have made what he will be* . . . "Not only is man what he conceives himself to be, but *he is* also *what he wills himself to be* after this thrust towards his existence. Man is nothing other than what he makes himself. Such is the first principle of existentialism."[19] Therefore, it can be easily observed that when Idealists believe in transcendental values, Naturalists believe that values are resident in nature, Pragmatists believe that values arise out of social life, existentialists affirm that the individual alone creates values. Reality is a state of becoming. Existence increases with every moment of life and essence is a consequence of this perpetual becoming.

Another significant concept of existentialism is the 'Contingency' of human life, the 'givenness' or 'thrownness'

(Dasien, being-in-itself of Sartre) of human life. Existentialists believe that existence of a person means his period from birth to death. There was nothing before birth and would be nothing beyond death. In between we have been thrown into a social life and the characteristics of this social life are the contingent circumstances of our life. This contingency is often characterised by experiences of dread, horror, anguish, solitude, bewilderment, uncertainty and finally limited by death.[20] It may be recalled that even Buddha recognised this contingency of human life as soon as he came out of his place and thus human suffering was the occasion of his philosophising. As Jean Wahl puts it : "Man is in this world, a world limited by death and experienced in anguish; is aware of himself as essentially anxious; is burdened by his solitude within the horizon of his temporality."[21] As such the whole gamut of metaphysics discussing about a transcendental being and purposes beyond death or an axiology discussing about transcendental values are mere imaginations of the mind designed to console an anguished soul and not the truth of existence. Alexander Koyre, in an informal discussion with Berdyaev, Gurvitch, Marcel, Jean Wahl and others describes in a very simple way the contingency of human life : "We are there; I am there such as I am; and I neither know why nor how; the only thing I know, truly and inexorably, is that someday I am going to die. And that is what limits all my possibilities and my future. My future limited, finite and I knowing it—that is my situation in the world. I know that my existence is precarious and short, and that I can lose it. This is the only thing that I have, and I can lose it at any moment; that is why there is the substratum of anxiety, fear and anguish."[22] Therefore, the sources, process and content of philosophising must be the situation in which one is placed. We are all aware of our situation in life, limited by death, and existentialists rightly remark that man is the only being in the world who knows that some time he will die. That is why his existence is throughout permeated by dread, anxiety and fear. He cannot escape or transcend this situation. He has to be prepared to face dread, anguish, axiety and fear resolutely and courageously. He must learn to live with anguish, dread and anxiety. He must learn to love death (just as Socrates, Lincoln, Kennedy, Gandhi and a score of other greatmen for whom dying for a meaningful cause was of greater significance than living a purposeless life). There are a number of correlates in Indian philosophy for existential concepts for *e.g.*, anguish: Dukha, dread and horror: Bhaya, Bhiti (Vita), etc. But when existentialism advises us to live with these categories of contingency, Indian philosophy counsels us to transcend them. This is very clearly evident in the concept of a *sthitha-prajna*[23] in the Gita. One sloka runs like this--

दु:खेशु मनद्विग्नः सुखेशु विगनस्पृह
वीतराग भय: क्रोध स्थितधि: मुनिरुच्छते ।।[24]

(He who is not depressed by anguish, elated by joy, and at times of fear, anxiety, love, horror and anger maintains his equanimity and poise is a sage).

Even the Indian attitude towards death is similar to that of existentialism. As an illustration, to quote Gita :

"संभावितस्य चाकीर्तिर्मणादतिरिच्छते"[25]

(For a man enjoying popular esteem infamy is worse than death). Gandhiji once had said that death in freedom is sweeter than life in bondage.

Another significant concept of existentialism is their view of man. In the age-long philosophical controversy of Free will *vs.* Determinism, existentialists prefer to view man as an infinitely free, responsible being. According to Sartre freedom is identical with existence.[26] As such existentialism has even been described as a search for ways in which man's freedom to create may be widely established and understood. In Marjorie Grene's terms : 'The revolutionary philosophy turns out to be philosophy of freedom—not just the philosophy of those who seek freedom but the philosophy of the very free act itself."[27] According to existentialists, man is not only free but he is condemned to be free. He is only not free, not to be free. This is the tragedy of human life. This infinite freedom entails upon him a heavy sense of responsibility, and this situation of being burdened with a heavy responsibility is the cause of dread, anguish and anxiety. The peculiar quality of human reality is that it is without excuse.[28] Man is always placed in a situation of 'Dharma Sankata'. A bold, honest, responsible and authentic existence would help man to face this situation.

Educational Implications of Existentialism

It is very difficult to discuss with a considerable degree of certainty and confidence about existentialistic education, as a good treatise on education by an existentialist is yet to appear. "The philosophy of existentialism has not displayed any particular interest in education."[29] Therefore, the educational implications that I discuss are those that are derived and deduced from their philosophy rather than those that are developed by existentialists. As Kneller feels: "Aside from casual references, such as those made by Kierkegaard and Marcel to their own schooling, existentialists, we repeat, do not carry their doctrine into practical theory or policy for school behaviour. We can only deduce curricular theory from philosophic doctrine helped here and there."[30] But I would like to discuss existentialist implications for education in a systematic way, of course supported by other sources.

Meaning of Education

In a broad sense education is that which helps an individual to realise the best that he is capable of.[31] In doing so education must help the individual to realise the 'facticity' (contingency) of his existence, to face the categories of this facticity—dread, anguish, anxiety and fear—resolutely and courageously and finally prepare him to meet death with pleasure. As such school life need not be a source of joy and happiness as for Rousseau, Froebel (Kindergarten) Pestalozzi and Montessori ('House of Happiness') or a place of training for social adjustment as for Dewey, but need to be permeated by dread and anxiety. The former type of education is unrealistic according to the existentialist. "Education for happiness is a dangerous doctrine because there can be no happiness without pain and no ecstasy without suffering."[32] Therefore, existentialists would welcome an education which throws open to children human suffering, misery, anguish and the dreadful responsibilities of adult life.

The world of education has hitherto been familiar with such concepts as education for complete living, for life, for happiness and for freedom. But existentialism speaks of a new kind of education—education for death. During and in between the two World Wars this concept of an education was uppermost in educational circles of United States, Germany, France and other European Countries where dying for one's own country constituted the supreme sacrifice. Students must develop a consistent scale of values, authenticate their existence by being committed to these values and so act as to be prepared to die for these values than to live without them. Brubacher presents a case for 'education for death' like this: "The attention given in our schools for education for death is 'grudgingly small' because death is regarded as a 'great misfortune'. This slighting of the study of death is anything but realistic, since history is replete with examples of self-sacrifice to the point of self-annihilation for the benefit of mankind."[33] But much depends upon the teacher and his understanding of his role which is very delicate as he has to cultivate simultaneously both the values of life and values of death. He must resourcefully point to the need for death for the sake of continuity of group life. He must make the child feel that it has conquered death. This can happen only when the child can say that life is cheap in comparison to some great cause.

Objective of Education

Existentialism believes, and rightly so from the point of view of psychology, that every individual is unique. Education must develop in him this uniqueness. In other words it must cater to individual differences. The objective of education is to enable every individual to develop his unique qualities, to harness his potentialities and cultivate his individualities. 'Non-conformity' is a desirable goal of education. Another belief of existentialists is that man is free by nature. As a corrolory, education must make pupil aware of the infinite possibilities of his freedom and the responsibilities he must bear in life. Education must also develop in him a scale of values consistent with this freedom. The pupil must develop a commitment to these values and act for them. In brief, "An uncompromising affirmation of authentic freedom and individual uniqueness is the message of existentialism for the philosophy of education today."[34]

Curriculum of Existentialism

Existentialists do not believe in prescribing a curriculum. The pupil must choose his own curriculum according to his needs, abilities and station of life. Though they agree to transmit some amount of fundamental knowledge about the universe in general, still they feel that the curriculum must be related to the immediate social, economic, political and other group problems which the individual will have to face. They emphasise that curriculum must be appropriated by the student and not just studied for an examination. It is not studying a subject but living, enacting and experiencing the values which are to be realied in learning that subject.

Existentialists give more importance to humanistic studies rather than for scientific subjects as it is through humanities that man comes to terms with human suffering, anguish, anxiety and death. Humanities help man to keep more closely to himself than sciences. Humanities represent subjective knowledge whereas sciences deal with objective knowledge. Self-knowledge precedes universal knowledge.

Methods of Teaching

Existentialists favour the Socratic approach to teaching as Socratic method is personal, intimate and an I—thou affair. Here knowledge and wisdom are gained through mutual interaction of two living beings. Methods of teaching must give more individual attention. That is why, at times, existentialists prefer better home education to school education. "For existentialism what counts is personal contact and not time-table."[35] As Kneller puts it: "The existentialist favours the Socratic method, not so much because it involves "induction" or the collection and analysis of all available evidence; nor because of its complementary process of 'definition', whereby general values are reached from particular instances; but chiefly because it is a method that tests the inner life—as a stethoscope sounds the heart."[36] But there must not be the least attempt at indoctrination. The teacher must never try to impose upon the children his ideas, ideals and values. Even religious education can be given provided there is no attempt at indoctrination. Methods of teaching must develop the creative abilities in children. 'Education for creativity', is most important for the existentialists.

Role of the Teacher

The role of the teacher in an existentialist scheme of education is very delicate. He must be the person who is himself authenticating his existence at every moment of his life, who has developed a consistent scale of values and committed to it. Without imposing himself he must make his children think about the problems of life. "If there is anything that the existentialist teacher can do for his students, it is to bring them to a more critical analysis and understanding of the meaning and purpose of existence, so that with time man may become more than a mere appetitive creature perpetuating the beștial habits of his simian ancestors."[37] For this, the teacher must treat his children as free individuals and sympathise with their rebellious nature. For, according to existentialists, a rebel is more moral than the conformist because he is authenticating his existence. There are no problem-children. Teachers must enter into the emotional life of children.

Critical Estimate of Existentialism

Existentialism has come into strong and pungent criticism from a number of philosophical quarters. It has been described variously as a form of 'metaphysical pornography', as one which 'encumbers the world of spirit', as 'over-stimulated, poisonous, perverse; a kind of swelling in the groin'. One of the severest critiques of existentialism Ruggeiro writes: "I believe that never before in the history of thought has such a radical nihilism been expressed, and what is more, with such impassivity and detachment. It is a philosophy of existence in which, between two nothings, we are given parenthetically life and the world, which is not a life or the world but a mirage of phenomenon that meet in a shiver of anxiety, in which the most exalted word of liberation lies in the recognition that the mirage is a mirage of nothingness."[38] But Ruggeiro, was a professor of philosophy at the University of Rome, a seat of Catholicism and this attitude in him towards existentialism is quite understandable. Sartre himself, aware of the criticisms against existentialism as an anti-humanistic philosophy wrote a book[39] to vindicate the humanistic spirit in existentialism where he has defended the same. As Kneller writes: "Sartre's defence and quasi eulogy of the French Resistance Movement and his indictment of prejudice in the 'Portrait of the Anti-semite' and 'The Respectful Prostitute', seem to indicate a profound sensitivity, for human suffering and a keen social awareness of cruelty, discrimination, and authoritarianism."[40] Even his book 'Of human freedom' contains the humanistic spirit in existentialism.

Conclusion

The only conclusion that author would like to draw about existentialism is that time is not ripe to conclude about existentialism. It is still a growing, young school of philosophy and we have to wait for some more time to draw conclusions. So, author would like to conclude this chapter by quoting Kneller: "The only safe conclusion to be drawn is that the last developments in this philosophic school are yet to be made and that all the avenues pursued by these men will be explored further and to some extent perhaps reconciled."[41]

REFERENCES

1. Kneller : 'Existentialism and Education', Phil. Library, N.Y., 1958, p. 19.
2. Jean Wahl : 'A Short History of Existentialism', Phil. Library, N.Y., 1949, p. 30.
3. Heidegger : "Existence and Being", Vision Press, London, 1949, p. 368.
4. Kenneth Richmond : "Socrates and the Western World"—An essay in the Philosophy of Education Alvin Redman, (Ed.) London (1954)., pp. 39-40, 46.
5. Gabriel Marcel "Man Against Mass Society", Henry Regnery Co., Chicago, 1952, p. 1.
6. Note : Having spent all his inherited property over his intellectual life and writing, Kierkegaard was "picked up in the streets and died in a hospital" at an early age of 43—vide *Runes* : "*Pictorial History of Philosophy*" Philosophical Library, New York, 1959, p. 227.
7. Ralph Harper : "Existence and Recognition" in NSSE 54th Yearbook. 'Modern Philosophies of Education' Part I, University of Chicago Press, Chicago, pp. 236-237.
8. There has been a misconception about the bonafides of existentialism as Heidegger and his philosophical uncle Nietsche have been wrongly associated with German National Socialism. It is a

matter of significance to note that Heidegger resigned from his rectorship of the University of Freiburg as he did not approve of Hitler's intentions and about Nietsche recent evidences in philosophical researches have shown that after Nietsche went insane in the last 12 years of his life, his unscrupulous sister, appropriated his manuscripts, tampered with them and spoiled the image of Nietsche. Vide *Runes* : Pictorial History of Philosophy, p. 301.

9. This approach to understand human nature has been pursued and called by Allport as the idiosyncratic approach ("Personality, Pattern and Growth" Holt, Rinehart and Winston, N.Y., p. 21. (Chapter I, 1963) and he enlists the admiration of all existentialists for this approach.

10. E.A. Allen : "Existentialism from within". R & K Paul, London 1953, p. 3.

11. (*a*) Hiriyanna : "The Aim of Indian Philosophy" In 'Popular Essays in Indian Philosophy', Kavyalaya Pubs., Mysore, 1952 p. 19.

    (*b*) Hiriyanna : "The Message of Indian Philosophy", Kavyalaya Publishers, Mysore, 1952, p. 37.

    (*c*) "A Sourcebook in Indian Philosophy" (Ed.) by Dr. Radhakrishnan and C.A. Moore, 'General Introduction', p. xxiv, Princeton University Press, N.J., 1960.

12. Aurobindo : "Essays on the Gita" Sri Aurobindo Ashram Pondicherry, 1970, p. 9.

13. Gita, Chapter I. Canto 35, Gorakhpur Press.

14. Dr. G. Srinivasan : "The Existentialists and Hindu Philosophical systems", Udayana Publications, Allahabad, 1967, p. 17.

15. *Ruggeiro*, "Existentialism" (Ed.) Happen Stall, Editor's introduction, p. 17, Secker and Warburg, London, 1946.

16. Sartre : "Being and Nothingness" (Dr.) H.E. Barnes Phil. Lib., N.Y., 1956 An abridged edition is available. "Condemned to Freedom" (Ed.) Justus Streller, Phil, Lib., N.Y., 1960.

17. H.J. Blackham : "Six Existentialist Thinkers', Macmillan Co., London, 1951.

18. Sartre : "Existentialism", The Philosophical Library, New York, 1952, p. 18.

19. Allport's conception of personality as 'Becoming' is worth recognising here. Allport : "Becoming—A Psychological Interpretation."

20. Heidegger's "Being and Time" is an exposition of this thesis.

21. Jean Wahl : *op. cit*, p. 31.

22. *Op. cit.*, Jean Wahl, p. 42.
23. K. Guru Dutt : "Existentialism and Indian Thought", Phil. Lib. N.Y., 1960, p. 18.
24. Gita, Chapter II, Gorakhpur Press.
25. Gita. Chapter II, Canto 33. Gorakhpur Press.
26. Sartre : "Of Human Freedom" (Ed.) W. Baskin, Phil. Lib., N.Y. 1966, p. 40.
27. Marjorie Grene : *Dreadful Freedom : A critique of Existentialism*, University of Chicago Press, Chicago, 1948, p. 25.
28. Sartre : *op. cit.*, p. 95.
29. J.D. Butler : "Four Philosophies and their practice in Education and Religion", (3rd ed.), Harper and Row, N.Y., 1968, p. 462.
30. Kneller : *op. cit.*, p. 122.
31. In a democrate education we have to add 'that may also be of social value'. But in existentialistic education we have to leave this out.
32. Kneller : *op., cit.*, p. 84.
33. Brubacher : "Education for death"—'School and Society', LVI, pp. 137-41. Aug. 22, 1942.
34. Kneller : "Contemporary Educational Theories" In "Foundations of Education" (Ed.), G.F. Kneller, John Wiley and Sons, N.Y., 1967, p. 121.
35. Niblett, W.R. : On Existentialism and Education", British Journal of Educational Studies. Vol. II, No. 2, May, 1954.
36. Kneller : *op. cit.*, "Existentialism and Education", p. 134.
37. *Ibid.*, p. 113.
38. Ruggeiro : *op. cit.*, p. 34.
39. Sartre : "Existentialism and Humanism", (Tr.) by Philip Mariet, Methuen and Co., London, 1948.
40. Kneller : *op. cit.*, p. 39.
41. *Ibid.*, p. 143.

CHAPTER 8

Language Analysis and Education

Meaning

Language analysis is relatively a new movement in the history of Philosophy and specially so in the field of education. As the title of the school suggests it is concerned with the analysis of language. It is an analytical approach to philosophy. Language analysis is purely a method and a technique to solve problems of philosophy and not a school of thought representing a metaphysical position about the universe, mind, man or such other phenomenon. It is concerned with the correct use of language to describe verifiable facts and ideas. It is also referred to as philosophical analysis or logical analysis. I would prefer to call it as the legal approach to education. The concern of language analysts about the correct use of words and phrases and about precise references is comparable only to legal situations and documentation. Usage for them has to be so precise and logical that A.J. Ayer views philosophy as 'a department of logic'[1] whereas the traditional philosophers consider it the other way.

History : When one traces the history of the movement one has to delimit one's scope to its organised form. However, if one likes to take pride in digging a hoary past for the movement then one can go as far back as Plato or Aristotle. One can go to the earliest attempts of analytical approaches to philosophy. For instance Kenneth M. Sayre argues that Plato drew out philosophy from its crude form towards a 'practicable method of philosophical analysis.'[2] Similarly, Urmson attributes the analytical quality to Aristotle as it is borne out in the latter's treatise 'Nichomachean Ethics'. As Urmson considers 'It is also the point of departure of analytic philosophy.'[3]

However, the origins of the movement in its present form has to be traced back to Ludwig Wittgenstein (1889-1951). He was born and brought up in Austria. Later he studied and taught at Cambridge. He was a student of Philosophy at Cambridge and studied under Bertrand Russell and G.E. Moore. Later he succeeded Moore as Professor of Philosophy at Cambridge University at a young age of thirty years. Initially Wittgenstein was very much influenced by Russell's philosophy of logical atomism. Logical atomism believed that complex problems and ideas can be conceived of or broken up into its minute or atomic form and can be solved with clarity later. Wittgenstein deviated from Russell in later years. He produced his monumental treatise : "Tractatus Logico Philosophicus' in 1921. The very next year it was translated into English. Being a revolt against the plethora of literature in Western philosophy it gained immediate and wide-spread popularity. Wittgenstein contended that the whole of Western philosophy and specially its metaphysical literature is nothing short of a veritable confusion of tongues. As he wrote : " .. most questions and propositions of the philosophers result from the fact that we do not understand the logic of our language."[4]

Wittgenstein felt that the language of common usage or ordinary language is defective and as such ineffective in either solving or dissolving philosophical puzzles. So he set himself the task of building up an ideal or perfect language. Quite a few philosophers in Cambridge became enthusiastic in supporting Wittgenstein's idea of the reconstruction of language or the creation of an ideal language to explain philosophical propositions. But there sprang up a group of philosophers at Oxford, prominent among them being J.L. Austin and A.J. Ayer who deviated from Wittgenstein's position that language analysis should coin new technical terms to solve philosophical problems. Rather they satisfied themselves in analysing ordinary language. They were referred to as Oxford group of language analysts. They were interested in analysing the innumerable terms used in philosophy such as Mind, Self, Value, Belief, Knowledge, Freewill, Good, Ought, Pleasant, etc. They confined themselves, to the examination of 'meaning' in philosophical propositions. This in brief is a sketch of the movement. As such there has not appeared a systematic and uniform history of the movement. There have been a few accounts here and there which overlap with each other. However, the two main trends : the reconstruction of an ideal language approach and the simple analysis of the ordinary language approach have stood out very clearly.[5]

In yet another development, there has appeared a corrective even to the ordinary language approach. It is felt that ordinary language is an outcome of attempts of groups of people to describe the objects, experiences, interactions, feelings, thoughts, etc., in their life-space. It is a medium of expression which has functional values. Ordinary language is fashioned on practical necessities. But this language may not be fool-proof as the perceptions of individual members of the group as well as the sub-groups within a larger group change and vary. Their understandings and styles of expression also change and vary. Hence it is only a guide for analysis and not the full substance. Concepts underlying usages in ordinary language should be analysed. This is a new thinking that may be called the 'conceptual analysis approach.' Prof P.H. Hirst of Cambridge University and Prof. R.S. Peters of London Institute of Education represent this approach. As they write : "Ordinary language is a record of connections and distinctions that men with predominantly practical purposes have found it important to make. It is, therefore, a valuable guide, but it should never be treated as a repository of unquestionable wisdom."[6]

Here I reproduce a personal communication received by me from Prof. P.H. Hirst in August 1978. These are his comments on the Chapter on Language Analysis in the first edition of this book. It represents the modern British thinking on Language Analysis and its implications for education.

"My main comment is that what you have characterised is not so much the nature of language analysis, philosophical analysis or logical analysis and education or *logical positivism and education.* The philosophical position of A.J. Ayer was certainly developed on the basis of Russell and the Wittgenstein of the Tractatus. It also rested on a form of analysis, but was above all a distinctive form of empiricism which had only limited and passing acceptance in philosophical circles even if the book was a great challenge. Very few have even accepted the verification principle in anything like his formulations and by the 1950s his whole position : anti-metaphysical, emotive theory of ethics etc,, was severely criticised. O' Connor's book is the only work in British Philosophy of education from Ayer's position, and has not been used for say, 15 years now. O' Connor's attitude to moral values and religious education plus his view of educational theory is almost universally rejected here nowadays. (I lie ! C.D. Hardie also did an 'Ayer' book !).

To most people here linguistic analysis is a label for a philosophical technique which in its early days was associated with logical positivism but from which it has long since cut completely free. The power of linguistic analysis is now seen as less (powerful) than was thought and it is employed now by people with Kantian or Aristotelian or other leanings. What is more, language itself is seen as but the way to examining concepts, meanings, forms of justification and so terms like 'philosophical' and 'logical' analysis are more appropriate. This is now (and has been since the 50's) here characterised by the work of the *later* Wittgenstein of the 'Philosophical Investigations' which almost totally rejects his earlier work of the Tractatus. Analysis is now the attempt to search for meanings in the use of language, accepting an endless variety of 'legitimate uses' in religion, morals, art, as much as in science and maths. The development of philosophy of education through Peters and Scheffler, above all, is characterised by *this* approach to analysis. It begins with 'ordinary' language, but does not regard that as necessarily the best language in which to make sense of ourselves and our world and experience.

So my reaction to your paper is that whilst I think it an interesting account of a brief period of philosophy of education under Ayer's influence, there is a need for another paper on what's happened since O'Connor's book. That's been dominated by analysis in a much wider, less doctrinaire sense ; it is *this* that has led to all the interesting work in the hey-day of philosophy of education here and in the U.S.A. under Peters and Scheffler. Nothing that you describe *really* characterises this later development very well—only its antecedents. To be fair Scheffler's 'Language of Education' was still very much under 'Ayer's influence'. Not so his later work. Peters is *very* anti-Ayer in all but certain techniques, and his conclusions are *totally* different for *e.g.*, on moral values, religion, nature of education, meaning."

Representatives. There are quite a few representative writers in the field. Mention may be made of only a few of them : Wittgenstein, J.L. Austin, A.J. Ayer, Israel Scheffler, Rudolf Carnap, Bertrand Russell, G.E. Moore, Gilbert Ryle and D.J.O. Connor, R.S. Peters and P.H. Hirst form only an illustrative list. Though Scheffler, Ryle and others have also written about education, D.J.O. Connor's "An Introduction to Philosophy of Education" was for some time a most comprehensive statement of the position of language analysts about education.

Main Philosophical Ideas. As language analysis is only a method of philosophy they have not built up any system of ideas or beliefs about the universe. In fact they are against any sort of systematisation. However, a few contentions of language analysis may be listed.

(*a*) Metaphysical statements about the world are neither true nor false but 'non-sense'. The world is the reality. The world for language analysts is that which is within the purview of sense-experience or that which is logically verifiable.

(*b*) The world is not determined by our perceptions. It is a real world which can be described only through a better use of language.

(*c*) Analytic method is the only method through which reality can be described. Philosophy is not a search for first principles. It is the act of analysis, criticism and clarification of the language used to describe reality. Speculation has no place in philosophy. Language analysis has little faith in the value of intuition though they are conscious of the limits of analysis. As Bertrand Russell writes : "They confess frankly that human intellect is unable to find conclusive answers to many questions of profound importance to mankind, but they refuse to believe that there is some 'higher' way of knowing, by which we can discover truths hidden from science and the intellect."[7]

(*d*) '......all statements about physical objects are indefinite.'[8] Any object can be described through a language. However much the perceiver attempts to describe his sense-data (physical object or experience) still he would have missed a part of it.

(*e*) Language analysts believe in cause and effect relationships, but only at the physical level.[9] They summarily dismiss the possibility of an ultimate cause as it is not verifiable.

(*f*) Value judgements pronounced by laymen through the use of ordinary language are usually defective. As such conditional statements which use 'if', 'in such a situation', 'under the defined circumstances', etc. need to be made while making value judgments.

Influence of Language Analysis on Education

The influence of the movement on educational thought and practice is profound and lasting. It is felt more unconsciously than one is conscious of it. Any work that begins with operational definitions, definition of terms used, and the like, bears the impact of language analysis. The research and writing on 'action research' and 'interaction analysis' in education may be conceived of as an effect of the movement. An examination of assumptions, exposure of logical fallacies, criticism, clarification and interpretation of educational concepts has by far helped to clear the debris in educational literature. Educational literature abounds with slogans and metaphors. An examination of these slogans has brought out the ambiguity and vagueness in them.[10] Scheffler has referred to a few such slogans while outlining the role of language analysis in education. He begins with a question and answers it himself thus : "What sort of landscape, then, does education present to the philosophical analyst ? Among its central concepts are such fundamental ideas as 'knowing', 'learning', 'thinking', 'understanding' and 'explaining' which figure prominently not only in the received philosophical literature but in ordinary affairs and in scientific psychology as well. In addition, there are much more specifically educational ideas as 'mental discipline', 'achievement', 'curriculum', 'character development' and 'maturity', which are intimately related to school affairs and are moreover, foci of continuing practical debate."[11] Analysis of educational situations has led to serious discussions among professionals in educational circles about the words they use, concepts they teach and facts they pass on. It is due to the movement that the format of the students' lesson plans in teacher education programmes has undergone and is still undergoing radical changes. I am unable to restrain myself from citing an interesting dialogue that prolonged for many days between two of my colleagues in a college where I was teaching about the statement of objectives in a lesson plan. One of them was advising his students to state them as : "the student develops the skills to..." while the other was following the format : "to develop the...skills in students." Obviously the quarrel was over the relative roles of the student and the teacher. The above experience is only illustrative. There arise many more such debates among teachers about the use of words in education. Another familiar discussion in teacher education programmes is this : 'Is teaching a profession ?' 'What are the criteria of a profession ?' etc.

Message to Teachers

Language analysis as a movement has a message to teachers. The message is about the "......right use of logic in analysing school situations, pupil behaviours, pupil performance, pupil-teacher and pupil-pupil relations, etc. "[12] Teachers should develop the habit of logical inquiry. It is not rare to meet teachers who conclude about the intelligence of a child on the basis of his performance in a particular subject and especially mathematics. Similarly teachers usually declare an aggressive and rebellious student as a juvenile delinquent. Many of the such decisions taken by the teachers and other educational practitioners would be irrational. A history teacher has to be quite analytical as fallacious generalisation in history develops defective attitudes in children. Teachers need to make 'meaningful' statements. Meaningful statements are those which are verifiable either empirically or logically. [Taken in this spirit, religious education would not find a place in the school curriculum of language analysts.][13]

Assessment of the Movement

'Language Analysis' is a movement that is still alive. One would not be able to achieve a desirable degree of objectivity in assessing a movement of one's own times. However, one cannot shut oneself up to the immense influence that language analysis brings to bear on one's everyday professional work. The influence of the movement has to be counted not in terms of the volumes added to philosophical literature by its writers but by the techniques they have shown us by which to discard a large amount of the volumes that are already there.

Clarity of thought and precision in communication ought to be prized possessions of any teacher. Language analysis emphasises primarily these qualities. Of course, there are a few writers who are disgusted with the importance given by language analysts to clarity in philosophical discussions. For instance Louis Arnold Reid writes : "The demand for clarity at every point has indeed been one of the paralysing obsessions of contemporary philosophy."[14]

REFERENCES

1. A.J. Ayer : "Language, Truth and Logic" *Gollancz*, London, (2nd Ed.), 1964, p. 57.
2. '*Plato's Analytic Method*', University of Chicago Press, Chicago, 1969, p. 238.
3. J.O. Urmson : "*The History of Philosophical Analysis*" in Richard Rorty (Ed.) : "The linguistic turn". The University of Chicago Press, Chicago, 1970, Phoenix Edition 1970, p. 294.
4. '*Tractatus Logico Philosophicus*', p. 63, Section 4.003, Kegan Paul, Trench, Trubner & Co., London, 1922.
5. For example, Richard Rorty has referred to the two approaches ; the ideal language approach and the ordinary language approach, in his introduction. In the same anthology Gustav Bergmann in his article "Logical Positivism, Language and the Reconstruction of Metaphysics" (p. 64) has referred to further variants such as the formalists, the reconstructionists, the pragmatists, the causists and the conventionists. A comprehensive history of the movement is yet to see the light of the day.
6. P.H. Hirst and R.S. Peters : "*The Logic of Education*", ELBS and R & K. Paul, London, 1975, p. 8.
7. "History of Western Philosophy", Unwin University Books, Allen & Unwin, London, 1969, p. 789.
8. A.J. Ayer : "Philosophical Essays", Macmillan & Co. Ltd, London, 1959, p. 140.
9. *op. cit.*, A.J. Ayer, p. 147.
10. B Paul Komisar and James Mc Clellan "*The Logic of Slogans*" in B Othanel Smith and Robert H. Ennis (Eds.) : "Language and Concepts in Education" Rand Mc Nally & Co., Chicago, 1961, pp. 195-214.
11. Israel Scheffler : *The Language of Education*" Charles C. Thomas, Illinois, 1960, pp. 8-9.
12. Richard Pratte : "Contemporary Theories of Education". IEP, London, 1971, p. 303.
13. There is an interesting article on the subject by W.D. Hudson : "Is religious education possible ?" In Glenn Langford and D.J.O.' Connor (Ed.) : "New Essays in the Philosophy of Education" Routledge and Kegan Paul, London, 1973, pp. 167-196.
14. "Philosophy and Education", Heineman, London, 1962, p. 11.

CHAPTER 9

Aims in Education

Most of the books on educational philosophy which discuss educational aims directly refer the reader to the subject proper. They discuss the various aims of education such as character development, citizenship training, self-actualisation, economic and social efficiency, national integration, democracy, international understanding, etc. Somehow they have missed, with honourable exceptions, either by intent or otherwise to discuss the very concept of an aim in education. Even the teachers of the subject often ignore it. As such most of the students of the subject fail to conceptualise the aims of education into a frame-work of action. Moreover it is incorrect to assume that they know about it or can do away with it. There is a need to know about the aims in education. Hence, the title of this chapter is not 'aims of education', but aims in education. It is proposed to discuss the foundations of aims of education in this chapter.

What do we mean by an aim in education ? Why should we have educational aims ? How are educational aims determined ? Should they vary according to time and place ? Are there any educational aims that transcend temporal and spatial limitations ? How is the determination of educational aims conditioned by varying social, economic and political factors, by differing philosophical and religious under-currents, by the conflicting psychologies of learning ? What are the criteria of sound educational aims ? These are some of the questions which a student of educational theory must be able to discuss with confidence. There may not be a foolproof answer to these questions. But one must be aware of the theoretical dimensions of the problem.

The need to be concerned about a discussion of aims in education is very pronounced and urgent in present times than it was in earlier times. In olden days there was no need to ask these questions. Philosophers defined the 'good' life and the 'good' society. Thus, they provided aims of education. Educators tried to realise the 'good' life and the 'good' society. But at present there has been such an enormous development in the realm of philosophy itself that there is not a single concept of good life and good society which can command universal acceptance. As Prof. Peters would say : "Nowadays philosophy has ceased to be a super-science of good and evil."[1] The traditional philosopher set out what ought to be. He was prescriptive. But the modern philosopher is analytic. Answers to questions on educational aims would be diverse and conflicting. Hence the need to study about aims.

Because of the analytic movement in educational philosophy a number of contradictions in the statement of educational aims have been brought to focus. For example, educationists, politicians and other public speakers proclaim that character development of children is a laudable aim of education. Supposing they are asked to describe in operational terms their concept of character, it is definite that they would come out with differing descriptions. There would be a communication gap between and among the educational theorists, policy markers, administrators and teachers about the meaning of character. Similarly many educators have said that 'complete living' should be the aim of education. But if a group of educators are ordained to delineate the constituents of complete living, they would not agree on a common list. Likewise there will be variation in the meanings of many of the aims of education that are familiar by now.

Another type of variation that warrants a discussion of the criteria of sound educational aims and moreover a priority among them is the proliferation of educational aims in the recent literature on education which are many a times conflicting with each other. As T P Nunn has put it: "Every scheme of education, being at bottom, a practical philosophy, necessarily touches life at every point. Hence any educational aims which are concrete enough to give definite guidance are correlative to ideals of life—and as ideals of life are eternally at variance, their conflict will be reflected in educational theories."[2] Therefore, to decide about the relative merits of conflicting interest groups and aims of education it is necessary to have a yardstick. A criteria of sound educational aims is such a yard-stick. It is necessary to set up the following questions to understand the role of aims in education.

What is an Aim of Education ?

All activities can be classified as aimed and aimless. A margin has to be given to the cynic who may argue that aimlessness itself is an aim. An activity which has a beginning, an end and an intervening process between the two can be said to have an aim. Dewey has defined an aim thus: "An aim implies an orderly and orderly activity, one in which the order consists in the progressive completing of a process."[3] Here, the word 'orderly' refers to the systematic nature of the activity. An aim gives a sense of order to the activity. The word 'ordered' refers to the direction implied in the activity. It influences the activity at each successive step. Therefore, an aim is that which gives a sense of order and direction to an activity. An aim means a foresight in advance, of the end, the consequences, the fruits of action. It is a foreseen end, it gives a direction to the activity and influences each step towards the end.

What are the Functions of an Aim in Education ?

An aim as a foresight of the end would help in the following ways :

	Necessitates observation of given conditions	means available for reaching the end, obstacles in the way
Foresight of the end	Suggests proper order or sequence in the use of means	To facilitate an economical selection and arrangement
	helps in the choice of alternatives.	

As the diagram above reveals, an aim helps in acquiring a reality-orientation, in the right choice of means and in realising economy of time and investment.

Why should we have an Educational Aim ?

"To have an aim is to act with meaning, not like an automatic machine."[4] There must be some meaning in the organised educational activities. Every activity ought to have a meaning which fits in progressively into a larger framework of meaning. It is only an idiot or an abnormal person who engages in a meaningless activity, who is not aware of the probable consequences of his actions, who is not able to visualise his activities in relation to other's activities. Aims are necessary to make life meaningful, purposeful and free of anxieties about consequences of action.

How to set up an Aim of Education ?

There are two apprcaches to answer this question. The first one refers to a general analysis of the method of setting up aims in the context of school life and the type of consequences it would lead to. The other refers to an analysis of the criteria of sound aims.

A. General Approach

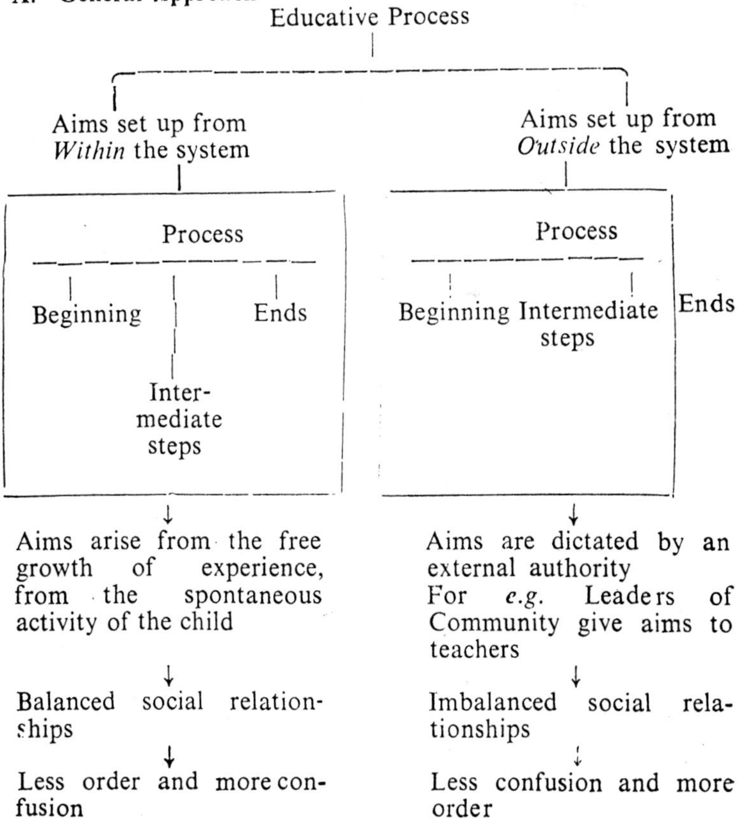

B. Criteria of Sound Educational Aims

1. Aims must emerge out of existing conditions. The social, economic and political conditions of a given group of people at a particular point of time must be kept in view while setting up aims of education. To illustrate, the Mudaliar Commission which submitted its report in 1952 had advocated the development of citizenship as an important and immediately significant aim of secondary education. This was a befitting aim for the existing conditions as India had just then achieved independance and declared itself as a Republic; it was necessary to build up an enlightened, socially and politically conscious citizenary. But by 1966, when the Kothari Commission submitted its report, it gave utmost importance to national development and to the solution of existing actue problems such as lack of self-reliance on the food front, unemployment and population control. As such an aim of education in the present times should keep track of the contemporary social, economic and political problems.

2. The aim should be only a plan of action, a tentative sketch, a blue-print. It must be flexible in character. One must be able to moderately deviate from it if necessitated by changing social, economic or politicial conditions. An aim that is exclusively dictated from outside the educational system tends to be rigid. External dictation, if required, must provide a broad framework of action only. Aim must be experimental in character; hence constantly growing as it is tested in action.

3. The aim must be founded upon the activities and needs of the given group of individuals to be educated. That is, it must depend upon the psychology of learning and development.

4. The aim should be defined, as far as possible, in operational terms. It should not be stated in a very general

and abstract way. It should lend itself for conceiving and formulating definite steps for its realisation. For instance, if it is said that the aim of education is to lead towards the 'Good life' or assist in 'Complete Living', and left at that, it would lead to confusion when a group of people try to formulate steps for realising the aim. There would be no general agreement about the concept of the aim.

5. The aim should reflect the individual and social aspirations of the people. It must be related to the 'life', needs and aspirations of the people. For example, the aspirations of the Indian people as declared in the constitution is to establish a democratic, socialistic, secular republic ; it is to achieve growth with social justice; the Constitution has defined through various articles and clauses the meaning of these terms. So education is a powerful means to realise the aspirations of the people as cherished in the Constitution. Aims of education should reflect the aims of national, social and individual life. Take another illustration, the aim of individual life, at its minimum, is to have a decent subsistence, successful social life and happy domestic life. Education must enable the individual to realise this aim.

6. The aim must always have a terminal point. The aim should be defined in such a way that after a stage there must be a termination of activities. For example, with this criterion in view if one looks at higher education in India at present one cannot stop wondering 'whither higher education.' If a student takes up the B. Sc. or B. A. course, then after the completion of the course he would have to reflect 'what next ?'. Then he may answer himself, 'let me take up M.A. or M.Sc.' in philosophy, history, psychology, Geology, Botany, Zoology, literature, etc. Again after M.A. or M.Sc. he will have to repeat his question 'what next ?' In many of these disciplines cited above, job opportunities are few and as such many of the

B.A's and B. Sc's or M.A's and M.Sc's are found to take up odd jobs which have little bearing on their education.

REFERENCES

1. R. S. Peters : "Must an Educator have an Aim ?" p. 83 in 'Authority, Responsibility and Education", Allen and Unwin, 1959, London.
2. T. P. Nunn: "*Education, Its Data and First Principles*", *op. cit.*, p. [illegible].
3. Dewey, John : "Democracy and Education", p. 102.
4. Dewey, *op. cit.*, p. 104.

CHAPTER 10

Individual and Social Aims in Education

The title of this chapter should be : the development of individuality as an aim in education in relation to the claims of the community or individual development *Vs* social efficiency as aims in education. However, considerations of euphony have suggested the above title.

Statement of the Problem

Throughout the recorded history of human civilisation there has been a perpetual discussion regarding the superiority of the individual over the society and that of the society over the individual. In fact the whole of the eventful history of mankind is a consequence of the relative emphasis on either the individual or society. There have been rival claims of individual and of society to occupy the 'fore-ground of the picture'. Whatever might have been the conclusions reached in such claims, the conclusions influenced the contemporary educational system. If it was conceded that individual was greater than society then education was for man and for himself. When society was considered as superior to the individual then education of man was for the service of the society.

It is interesting to understand the consequences of accepting either of these ideologies on education and identify and analyse the attendent dangers of taking these to their extremities. By such a process of analysis it is possible to find whether there is a real antithesis between the individual and social aims of education or is it only a matter of emphasis (difference in the degree of stress). In the latter case a synthesis can be achieved, but in the former—when the rival claims are taken to their extremity—reconciliation is impossible.

(Thesis) : Social Aim in Education

Man is essensially a social animal. He is born into a social heritage. He has become what he is due to the influences upon him of other social beings—parents, teachers, schoolmates, brothers, sisters, friends, enemies, employers, colleagues, etc. Therefore, he is only a unit of a larger whole 'Society'—usually the State. He can live as an individual only because he is in a society. Man enjoys the facilities of health, housing, food, education, transport, communication and so many other comforts of modern living which cannot be enumerated exhaustively. He enjoys these comforts only because of his membership in an organised society.

Inference

In return to the care, comforts and protection that society gives to an individual he has to surrender all his rights to the well-being of the society. The interests of the society in which the individual lives are superior to his personal interests. He must seek his welfare through the promotion of the social good. Though such a thinking was not new to the world, still in 1851, Thomas Hobbes paraded and popularised it in his treatise on the commonwealth of nations : 'Leviathan'. The thesis of the book is that the State, a society, is a gigantic entity, whereas the individual is only a puny entity before the State. Therefore, the individual must submit himself to the State. Later the German Philosopher Hegel idealised the State in his philosophy of dialectical idealism. He considered the State as a superpersonal spiritual entity. As Ross puts it : "The State is conceived of as an idealised metaphysical entity, over and above the individual citizen, superior to him in every way, transcending all his desires and aspirations. It is the embodiment of all reason and justice ; it has a mission and a destiny to fulfil, and it is conscious of that mission and destiny."[1] As such the individual's activities should be directed towards the realisation of the mission and destiny of the State. Public service or the service of the State is the highest good of life.

Impact on Education

State will have absolute control over the life and destiny of each individual. State will make education a powerful means of achieving its end. Education will only be a potent tool. The State enforces a rigid system of State-education, a uniform education; it shall reserve the supreme right to dictate what shall be taught and how it shall be taught. Obedience, discipline, submission to authority, attitude of service to the State are the watchwords. Education is for social efficiency. As Ross puts it : 'The authorities seek to judge how best he will serve the State, and they train him for that end. Educational opportunities are given on the basis of the suitability of the person to serve the State."[2] Therefore, the poor and the handicapped cannot claim education as a right.

Illustrations of the practice of social aim in its extreme form :

1. Ancient Sparta provides the perfect paradigm of an extremely socialised State. Plutarch, considered as the original law-giver of Greece, gives an account of Spartan life in his "Life of Lycurgus." In Sparta 'each man was not born for himself, but for his country.' He 'had not a wish but for his country.' Newly born children were examined for their physical fitness. Weaklings were exposed to on the mountain-side. It was a case of perfectly logical savagery.

State itself was a school. Education was geared to military training. Immediate aim of education was to make soldiers out of pupils. Education was 'calculated to make pupils subject to command, to endure labour, to fight and conquer.' Their whole education was an 'exercise in obedience.' Even the literary education comprised of patriotic songs from Homer, praises of heroes who had died for Sparta and condemnation of those who had declined to fight. However, women were given importance as they were mothers of future warriors. As a result it is said that "Sparta was well prepared for a life at times of war. But it rusted like a sword in the scabbard at times of peace."

2. In recent times, both before and after the first world

war a similar philosophy of the State was preached as well as practised in Germany. Fichte emphasised that education is the most potent tool to realise the ideals of the State. Then Hegel idealised the State. The combined effect of such a philosophy was the rise of Nazi Germany. In Nazi Germany, individuality was damped down at every stage ; press was dictated ; foreign newspapers and broadcasts were suppressed ; unquestioning loyalty and obedience to the Feurer and the Nazi party was exalted. The individual was only a cog in the wheel.

(Anti-Thesis) : Individual Aim in Education

The interest of the individual are supreme and superior to that of the society. It is only because of individuals that a society is there. Social institutions exist only for the well-being of the individual. Social institutions are necessary for personality—formation. But the personality of the individual overrides the importance of the institutions which form it. The material to be moulded is more important than the mould itself. "National traditions are important only because they help to fashion desirable patterns of individual life."[3] They are there to make his life better, fuller, richer, happier, secure and fruitful. The individual is greater than society because "Nothing good enters into the human world (society) except in and through the free activities of individual men and women."[4] All great men were free individuals.

Impact on Education

The State is there only to provide opportunities through its schools to develop individual potentialities. It can exert control over the schools in a general way rather than in a detailed fashion ; there is no rigidity in the curriculum and methods of teaching. System of education provides for equal opportunities ; for instance poor, handicapped, minorities and lower class students get scholarships and other facilities. Education is not an exclusive right of a privileged class, by virtue of wealth, caste, intelligence, etc. Education must secure for everyone 'the conditions under which individuality is most completely developed.'

What is individuality ? It is an ideal, the attainment of which is the end of life and education. It is a potentiality which education has to make as an actuality. Individuality is not eccentricity. As T P Nunn puts it : "The primary aim of all educational effort should be to help boys and girls to achieve the highest degree of individual development of which they are capable of."[5] The educative process which tries to realise this aim will be characterised by freedom of belief, expression and behaviour. Individual liberty is highly valued. Curriculum will be flexible. There will be scope for experimentation.

Limitation of Individual Aim

Society may at times of crises, demand services that entail the suppression, even the final sacrifice, of individual development. To illustrate with examples from India, emergency was declared during Indo-China war, Bangla-Indo joint war with Pakistan and in 1975 it was declared to maintain political and economic stability in the country. During the times of emergency, when it has been 'genuinely' imposed, individuality has to be submitted for social good. But individual may mistake liberty for licence. Usually individual will be more conscious of his rights than of his duties. That is why in the recent Constitutional amendment in India there is a definition of duties of the Indian Citizen.[6]

Synthesis between Individual and Social Aims

The individual and social aims are complementary rather than being contradictory. Individuality has a meaning only in a social context. It also develops in a social atmosphere. The difference between man and individual is that man is raw form of the species, a product of natural development ; whereas individual is man-in-society.

Individual and social aims are only two dimensions about the same phenomenon, life. Supposing a cup is half full with water, both the persons who say it is either half full or half empty are correct. One cannot deny that 'Good of each is Good of all.' Neither can one refuse to accept that 'Good of all is Good of each'. It is only a difference in the degree of emphasis or approach for action. There is no conflict between self-realisation and social service as aims of life and education. The aim of individual development should be social service. Gandhiji used to say 'I see God in every human being, therefore, service to humanity is service to God.' His philosophy has been described as humanistic idealism. One cannot think of individual development which will not in some way or the other, directly or indirectly help for the social Good. To illustrate, for a teacher, individual development means to be a 'Good' teacher. A teacher becomes a 'Good' teacher only when his students (mainly), his colleagues, his superiors and the community in which he works, in short his society accept him to be so. 'Goodness' of a teacher has a social connotation. Even 'Greatness' is a social concept. All individual qualities that go to make up character of an individual are social in nature. Similarly the adjectives used to describe the behaviour, abilities, attainments, etc : of an individual bear a meaning in a social context. As Ross puts it ; "Individuality is of no value and personality is a meaningless term apart from the social environment in which they are developed and made manifest. Self-realisation can be achieved only through social service, and social ideals of real value can come into being only through free individuals who have developed valuable individuality. The circle cannot be broken."[7]

There are a few illustrations of societies which attempted at a reconciliation of the individual and social aims of life. One of them is the ancient Greek city of Athens at the time of Pericles. There was generally high level of social welfare, prosperity and peace ; even from the point of individual development, there were quite a few individuals who distinguished themselves in different walks of life————————————, ————, —————, —————, ——————, are only a few names to cite. It is said that ancient Greek society witnessed its golden age during the reign of Pericles. Similarly Indian society is recorded to have witnessed its golden age during the reign of Chandragupta the Second. The historically famous 'Navamanies' were his contemporaries and courtiers.

Impact on Education

Education has to be designed and administered in such a way that each individual has to develop to the fullest extent his abilities and realise his potentialities, and simultaneously develop an attitude to put these abilities into the service of others. As T. P. Nunn puts it : "Educational efforts must be limited to securing for everyone the conditions under which individuality is most completely developed—that is, to enable him to make his original contribution to the variegated whole of human life as fully and as truly characteristic as his nature permits."[8]

Individual and Society are two ends of a continuum called

life. Education has to recognise the limits of this continuum and maintain a harmonious balance between the two.

REFERENCES

1. Ross : 'Groundwork of Educational Theory', p. 37.
2. Ross, *op. cit.*, p. 38.
3. T. P. Nunn, *op.* cit., p. 4.
4. T. P, Nunn, *op. cit.*, p. 4.
5. *Op. cit.*, p. 5.
6. Indian Constitution, 43rd Amendment.
7. Ross, *op. cit.*, p. 52.
8. *Op. cit.*, pp. 5-6.

CHAPTER 11

Democracy and Education

A study of the relation between democracy and education would be of special interest in a democratic political organisation of society. Development and Promotion of democratic citizenship is of primary concern to educators in a democracy. Democracy as a form of political and social organisation has a glorious past. The ancient Greeks were practising a type of democracy. Aristotle in his treatise on politics refers to three forms of government.[1] Even in those times he collected the constitutions of most of the countries then known to the Greeks, analysed them and identified the three forms of government. His format is presented here :

Political Organisation

- Rule by one
  - Monarchy Dictatorship
  - Benevolent Despotism
- Rule by a few
  - Oligarchy
  - Aristocracy
- Rule by many
  - Mobocracy
  - Democracy

One cannot think of any political organisation which escapes this classification.

Meaning of Democracy

Democracy has many connotations as applied to different spheres of life such as the political, social and moral spheres. From the point of view of political organisation it has been defined as rule by the people, for the people and of the people. As a social organisation democracy means sharing of power, responsibility, experiences, joys and sorrows. Each of these meanings touch one or the other aspects of democracy and not its essence. In fact democracy cannot be defined in a comprehensive way and in its entirety. It can only be described. William Walsh would say that philosophically : "Democracy is a way of life, a way of doing things, which penetrates deeply every phase of life's practical affairs."[2] If democracy is a way of life, communism can be claimed to be a way of life. So, the question is : What characterises and distinguishes democracy as a way of life ?

The personality of the individual is judged as supreme and

of measureless worth. It is also an order of social relationships among individuals which is dedicated to the promotion of the individual well-being without sacrificing collective interest. It can be viewed as the spirit of understanding, sympathy and co-operation in recognising the worth of every individual. It envisages a responsibility for every individual and a belief in such responsibility as the cause of progress and welfare of humanity. It is a society in which every individual will get adequate opportunities to blossom according to his potentialities and in which power and responsibility are shared. As Dewey writes : "A democracy is more than a form of government, it is primarily a mode of associated living, of conjoint communicated experiences."[3] It is that way of life where problems are solved through argument, discussion and persuation instead of dictation, coercion and violence.

A Priori Faiths of Democracy

(*a*) Faith in the dignity and worth of human personality : The fundamental difference between democracy and any other form of political organisation is that in the final analysis the individual (and his interest) is superior to the society (State) in which he lives. Individual is an end in himself and not a means. He is not an economic or social unit. As such the individual should not be used as an instrument in the hands of the State and his interest should not be made to subserve the interests of the State. The individual should be allowed the freedom to choose duly respecting the freedom of other individuals also. In short the State exists for the individual and depends upon his judgments for its functioning.

(*b*) Democracy believes that the earth and its resources belong to the human race and not any individual or a group of individuals. Even a portion thereof belongs to all those people who inhabit it. Therefore, all individuals share an equal quantum of essential human heritage. All men are created equal and therefore, all are equal before law and are entitled to the same treatment before law. Equal opportunity includes social, economic and political equality.

In general it means that no person shall be denied the chance to share in the good of the society by reason of his race, religion, caste or nationality. The access to opportunity for all the citizens will be the same instead of providing arbitrary privilege for some and depriving others of the same. It assures only an equal chance of success and not equal success. Equality of opportunity is not identity of opportunity. It only means that discrimination, if any, in the distribution of opportunities is only based on individual abilities and potentialities and not on birth, breed, creed, caste, class, race or religion. Rather allowances are also made, for the social, economic and other handicaps that influence performance, while distributing opportunities. This is variously described as 'protective discrimination', 'reverse discrimination', 'affirmative action' or 'positive discrimination'.

Freedom of Inquiry

Freedom to inquire is a corollary of both the rational nature of man and the fundamental right that he derives from democracy-freedom. Referring to the former, Aristotle had conceived of man as a rational animal and Des Cartes went to the extreme in telling "I think, therefore, I am." Rousseu had referred to the latter when he said : "Man is born free, (but every where he is in chains)."[1] In the context of political life Tilak had said that "Freedom is my birthright." Freedom of inquiry is essential for the continuity of democracy. It is said that 'eternal vigilance is the perpetual price of democracy.' Such vigilance is possible only in a free society of inquiring minds. It is not the copying mind but the reasoning mind that inquires.

Freedom is not an end in itself. It is only a means to the improvement and further development of the democratic ideals which remain open to scrutiny. Freedom of inquiry should not be aimed at the destruction of democracy. There is a scope for the all individuals to think independently, discuss with each other, arrive at a consensus and act collectively, rather than subject themselves to the dictates of any single individual or a group therein. The conclusions arrived at will be open to scrutiny and revision in the light of subsequent developments, additional information or evidences and improved data gathering instruments.

Faith in the Educability of Man

Democracy believes that all men educable. Through education they acquire the capacity for self-direction and self-improvement. All types of persons including deaf and dumb, handicapped and mentally retarded will get a fair deal. The voice of every individual will have its weight. Education will improve the quality of the people and they would be better able to participate in the affairs of the group.

Self-Criticism and Self-Evaluation

Democracy believes that nothing is perfect, including democracy—hence the need for criticism. One of the strikingly significant green-spots of democratic principles is the very openness of democracy for self-criticism and self-evaluation. Criticism involves the ability to discuss, discern and judge. But this criticism is founded on the fundamental and optimistic premise that democracy is right and good, that it will both survive and progress in an environment which welcomes continuous criticism and perpetual evaluation. For instance 'press' is one of the most important watch-dogs of democracy. Democracy offers maximum opportunities for self-criticism and self-evaluation through the press. Criticism and Evaluation are necessary for strengthening and vitalising the purposes for which democracy stands.

Creativity and Change

The ideals of democracy are based on the faith that life is subject to change and that this change may be directed in desirable ways and towards the welfare of all the people. Change is basic for the survival and progress of democracy. Sometime change may be for the good. Other times it may not be so. But it is always the collective will that decides about the change. The various amendments to the constitution witnessed so far including the 42nd constitutional amendment which touched the fundamental rights is symbolic of this faith in change. So far there have been 59 amendments to the Constitution. How the best war-time Prime Minister of England, Churchill, was brought down from power immediately after he had won a great war for England, the second world war, and Atlee contesting from the rival political group, the labour party was elected to power, is a burning illustration of the faith of democracy in change.

Democracy implies growth and adjustment to changing needs and not a propagation of its ideas. Though it likes to be stable still it is not a static but a dynamic stability that is the good of democracy. The only and sure test of an idea in a democracy is determined by how it survives the competition of rival ideas, studied and presented freely. Hence democracy places a lot of premium on creative thinking that leads to successful experimentation and improved growth.

Education in a Democracy

Just as it is under any other form of political organisation, even in a democracy, education preserves, perpetuates and promotes the ideals of democracy. Through these functions it enables democracy to achieve social control, social stability and social progress respectively. Education in a democracy gives scope for actual experiencing of the functioning of democracy through participation, self-expression and discussion.

It has been universally recognised that the strength of democracy depends upon the character and intelligence of all its citizens. As Dewey puts it ; "The devotion of democracy to education is a familiar fact. A government resting upon popular suffrage cannot be successful unless those who govern and obey their governers are educated."[5] Democracy offers immense freedom for the individual. It is only education that helps him to interpret freedom in terms of responsibility. Freedom means responsibility. They are the two faces of the same coin. Thomas Jefferson had said : It is impossible for man to be both free and ignorant. In a sense ignorance is bondage whereas knowledge is freedom. As Plato had said : 'A slave is one who accepts from another the purposes which control his conduct.' Bernard Shaw highlights the value of education in a democracy in his characteristic satirical fashion thus : Democracy implies election of the corrupt few by the ignorant many. Therefore, education is the major means to enrich the strenghs and overcome the weaknesses of the people. It is also a means for the widespread diffusion of democratic values.[6]

Objectives of Democratic Education

Education in a democracy should try to develop the following loyalties in children.

(*a*) To himself as a human being of dignity and worth. This implies not only a self-regard or the attitude of valuing one's liberty but also recognising the right of other people to value their dignity and worth.

(*b*) To the principle of human equality and brother-hood.

(*c*) To a belief that political, social and economic problems are best solved through non-violent and peaceful methods like arguments, discussions, negotiations and persuasions instead of violent, anti-social, corrupt and treacherous methods.

(*d*) To the ideal of honesty and fair-play in the solution of social problems and to develop a scientific attitude of mind which is characterised by balance of temper, suspended judgment, etc.

(*e*) To the ideal of respect for and appreciation of talent, training, character and excellence in all fields of social endeavour.

(*f*) To the obligation and right to work.

(*g*) To duly constituted authority—may it be in social, political, professional or any other walk of life.

(*h*) To the obligation to be socially sensitive and informed; that is, to continuously educate oneself.

Curriculum in a Democracy

The values cherished by democracy are largely realised

through the curriculum of the schools. The curriculum in a democracy should be as flexible as possible so as to meet the individual needs of children. The characteristic feature of democratic education is that it allows for maximum individual development and this is possible only through a flexible curriculum that can cater to the diverse tastes and talents, needs and interests, abilities and aptitudes. Curriculum must be punctuated by flexibility, elasticity and variety. Curriculum should not be something which can be used to 'teach democracy' but enable one to 'live democracy'. Curriculum must be framed in the form of problems for discussion wherever it is possible to do so.

Methods of Teaching in a Democracy

Democracy encourages group methods of teaching. Project method, group discussions, problem—solving are all approved by it. Learning by living (doing) is emphasised. The school is considered as the laboratory to practice democracy. There is no scope for mechanisation and indoctrination. Pupil initiative is always encouraged. Methods of teaching should develop rational thinking and reflection in children. Discussion of controversial issues is very much encouraged.

Role of Teachers in a Democracy

The role of teachers in a democratic scheme of education is crucial. Teachers ought to be embodiments of all the values cherished by democracy. They must exemplify in their conduct and behaviour the outcomes of education contemplated by democracy. Children 'catch' democracy from teacher easily rather than they learn it through studying about it.

Teachers should be democratic and human in their outlook,

more so in their behaviour. They should be objective, that is free from prejudices and favouritism. They have to encourage pupil—initiative. They have to allow children to put questions and discuss with them, rather, stimulate them to do so. They should be discerning in the use of authority and in providing freedom to children. They are to create an atmosphere where children are self-disciplined.

Limitations of Democracy

There may arise many problems in the practice of democratic education. These problems may emerge out of defective implementation of democratic principles instead of being inherent in the system itself. Some of them are listed here :

(*a*) Misgivings as to the spirit of democracy : an imbalance in emphasis between collective *versus* individual interests would lead to lopsided development in children. Individual interests may reign over social or group interests and thus lead to unfair exploitation ;

(*b*) Ignorance or insufficient awareness of social values, and consequently imbalanced social relationships ;

(*c*) Absence of common loyalties to the group: personal and vested interests that conflict with each other ;

(*d*) Practice of demogogy; people who are incapable of critical thinking are susceptible to demogogy and they are usually more in number.

(*e*) Indoctrination : Teachers with rigid views, strong likes and dislikes may impose their views or try to promote them which is against the spirit of democracy.

REFERENCES

1. Aristotle : "Politics"
2. "Education and Political Power" Ch. V.
3. Dewey, John : "Democracy and Education", p. 87.
4. J.J. Rousseau : "Social Contract", p. 1.
5. John Dewey : "Democracy and Education" The Macmillan Co., N.Y., 1944, p. 87.
6. For a detailed and useful description of democratic education refer to "Learning the ways of Democracy" Educational Policies Commission NEA, U.S., 1940.

CHAPTER 12

National Integration as an Aim of Education

India after independence has not reflected a steady and continuous sense of national solidarity. It has been a relatively stable society with longer periods of peace than turmoil. However, there have been occasional outbursts of linguistic chauvinism, communalism, political upheavals, inter-State disputes and the like which had assumed national proportions and attracted wide attention. On the other hand there have also been occasions when in times of crises due to both external forces such as foreign aggression and internal forces such as political instability, famine and flood, Indians have displayed a tremendous sense of unity. But national solidarity in India is unevenly punctuated by events which though initially appear to be insignificant still at a later stage almost paralysed the normal functioning of society. As such national integration is a highly significant aim of education. Before discussing the aim in all its details it would be interesting to ponder a little while over the question : Is India a nation ? There have been both negative and positive answers to this question. For instance, Sir John Strachey had said : "This is the first and most essential thing to learn about India—that there is not and never was an India or even any country of India, possessing according to European ideas, any sort of unity ; physical, political, social or religious : No Indiau nation, no 'people of India' of which we hear so much."[1] Even Mohammed Ali Jinnah had said at the time of partition, while publicising his two-nation theory : "There is no such thing as one Indian nation ; there are two nations—the Hindu nation and the Muslim nation." He did not conceive of India as a heterogeneous group beyond its religious dimension.

There are also the other type of views which considered India as a nation. The famous British Historian Vincent Smith who was the first to write the history of India in the English language wrote as early as 1906 : "India beyond all doubt possesses a deep underlying fundamental unity far more profound than that produced either by geographical iso lation or by political suzerainty. The unity transcends the innumerable diversities of blood, colour, dress, manners and sect."[2]

Dr. R.P. Singh : "India represents a macrocosmsic unity in a microcosmic diversity."[3]

Many more similar opinions may be presented either for or against the view that India is a nation. But it is difficult to judge on rational grounds whether any of these opinions have any sense or not, though the question can be answered easily on sentimental grounds either way. These opinions drive us to another fundamental question : What is a nation ? Here are a few selected definitions of a nation.

Stalin : "A nation is a historically evolved stable community of language, territory, economic life and psychological make-up manifested in a Community of Culture."[4]

Dr. S. Abid Hussain : "An ideal nation is one which has a "domicile in a compact geographical area, unity of race, religion, language and general culture and a common history."[5]

Dr. N.V. Thirtha : "A nation may be supposea to exist if the people living under an established political authority and order accept for themselves a common destiny in terms of the mutual benefits that individuals or groups of individuals may be deriving or hope to derive."[6]

Nicholas Hans has enumerated five factors in his book "Educational Tradition" which go to make up an ideal nation.[7] They are : (*a*) unity of race, (*b*) unity of religion, (*c*) unity of language, (*d*) compact territory and (*e*) political sovereignity. Quite a few illustrations can be cited of nations recognised to be so and which are successful that refute Han's definition of nation. However, he himself admits that one or many of these factors may be lacking without seriously endangering the unity of national culture. In spite of this, to illustrate a few cases : Unity of race is conspicuous by its absence in the United States but still it is a nation ; Belgium has 2 national languages but still it has remained a nation ; many of the European countries such as Holland are divided by religion but they are also nations ; Poland was deprived of its political sovereignity for over a century as it happened to many countries ruled by the British or the French but

Poland has remained a nation ; the West Indies is a group of islands without compact territory but it is also a nation ; further, India is also a nation where there are many religions and national languages.

The illustrations cited above highlight the limitations of any definition of a nation. In a simple way a nation can be said to be a group of men living under an established political order and moving towards common goals. A 'nation' is only an ideal. It never is, it is always becoming. So the question whether a particular country *X* is a nation or not is meaningless and hence to be dismissed. The sensible question would be to ask whether the country *X* is moving towards common goals, if so, then it is becoming a nation. And, in the history of any country common goals would always be changing so as to meet the changing environment.

National Integration in India

It is interesting to ask whether India is politically, socially, economically and culturally a stable society. From the functional or operational point of view one would be prompted to answer the question that it is so, but not to a sufficient degree. If the objective of national integration means "bringing about economic, social and cultural differences within a tolerable range" then India has to do a lot more about it to realise that. In doing so it has to fight the barriers towards the goal and also consolidate the favourable forces.

Barriers for National Integration

There are a number of identifiable and not so easily recognisable factors that operate against national integration. By nad large these factors are expressions of self-centred groups with vested interests. Some of them work as under-currents which do not come to the surface and hence not noticeable. Those which can be easily noticed and labelled are discussed here :

(*a*) *Race*. Racial diversity has not been a source of social conflict in India to the extent it has been in some other parts of the world. Morever race in its pure stock does not exist in India. However, the racial origins of the people of India can be traced back to the Indo-Aryans, the Dravidians and to some extent the Mongolians. Even now the racial sentiments are played up. For instance, the Dravida Kajhagam Party of Tamil Nadu for which the Dravida Munnetra Kajhagam was the political wing staged a row against what they call the Aryan domination of Indian culture. In fact, they burnt the epic poems Ramayana and Mahabharatha which are revered as sacred by a large section of the Indian masses. But this was only a passing phase but not a permanent feature of the Indian social life.

(*b*) *Language* : Language has been one of the strongest threats to the stability of the nation. There are nearly 900 dialects out of which 850 dialects are spoken by less than a lakh of persons. Non-Indian languages also have currency in the country. However 95 per cent of the Indian population fall under one or the other of the 16 national languages which are declared so according to the 8th Schedule of the Indian Constitution. Because of the vastness of the land, India has not been able to settle upon a language so far which can be taken as the link language for official purposes. Mere indications of attempts to evolve a link-language, for instance Hindi, which is spoken by majority of the population in the country, has led to wide spread violent reactions. Occasions were many when normal life was paralysed, public property was destroyed, arson, looting and criminal acts were committed in the name of language. Language has become a strong disintegrating force of Indian social life. Even the States of India were reorganised on linguistic basis so as to solve this problem. But it has not been able to completely solve the problem. Regionalism as an evil force centres largely around language. The Shiv Sena movement led by Bal Thakre in Maharashtra is only an apparent illustration of such sentiments. Such regional groups which play on linguistic sentiment exist in most of the Indian States today.

(*c*) *Cultural Differences* : There are a number of other cultural differences that also are potential threats to the solidarity of the nation. Some of them are the caste and subcaste consciousness among the people, practice of untouchability, religious diversities (Punjab problem) etc. A discerning observer of Indian socio-political life would be able to identify many more sources of disintegration and it is not necessary to go into those details.

(*d*) *Economic Disparities* : Such disparitics exist between and among the States of India, among the districts in a State, and among the blocks in a district. Economic backwardness leads to emotional unnest between regions (Gorkha land agitation), among social groups.

Favourable Forces for National Integration

There are a number of geographical, historical and socio-political forces that contribute to the stability of India. Even the high school text books discuss the geographical and historical factors that have given a sense of unity to the nation. In recent times that is after independence, the development of tourism, the carrying of science and technology to rural areas and the like have strengthened the previously existing sense of unity in the country. A common constitution, federal set up, national symbols and songs etc., have also helped in this regard.

There are also a number of cultural values that have held the nation as a strong and stable unit in spite of the vicissitudes arising out of foreign invasions, internal squabbles and anti-social trends. Tolerance, as a value of life is only an illustration. Tolerance is not indifference. Highlighting the place of tolerance in Indian life Jawaharlal Nehru has thus said : "Some kind of a dream of unity has occupied the mind of India since the dawn of civilisation. That unity was not conceived as something imposed from outside, a standardisation of externals or even beliefs. It was something deeper and within its fold, the widest tolerance of belief and custom was practised and every variety acknowledged and even encouraged."[8] Apart from tolerance, there are also other modern values such as democracy, socialism and secularism, the emerging awareness of which is most favourable to the building of a strong unified and integrated India. Thus, there is already an undercurrent of strong potential to bring about unity in Indian social life. But this has to be lifted to the surface and those who live this social life must be made aware of this.

Reasons for the Delay in the Process Towards National Integration

Every society can be thought of as a system comprising two sub-systems, the maintenance system and the projective system. The projective system refers to the values, customs, traditions, norms, beliefs and behaviour-patterns whereas the maintenance system refers to the application of science and technology in daily life, mass communications and transportation and such other artefacts of life. The two systems correspond to the conceptual and functional tiers of society. It is commonly observed that the maintenance system moves faster than the projective system. For instance, it may be observed that even though people may use buses, cars, telephones, electrical gadgets and appliances, still they have not given up the practice of untouchability, sanctity or prudence in daily life, over-consciousness of caste and sub-caste relationships, etc. The differential speed between the maintenance and the projective system in a society leads to a 'gap' or a 'lag' which has been called as the culture lag. Culture lag gives rise to problems of social cohesion. Bridging this culture gap is a perpetual process. Hence, at no time in the history of a society can permanent stability or integration of social or national life can be brought about. It is said in this sense that a nation never 'is', it is always 'be coming'.

Culture lag poses a number of problems of adjustment to the people. One of them is the development of a centrifugal attitude, expecially among some of the elite in the community who in their eagerness to overcome the lag, despise loyalty to the nation and owe their loyalty to the world at large. They are extremely broad-minded and over-bearingly cosmopolitan in outlook. Another contrasting problem is the development of centripetal attitudes in people. This is characteristic of half-educated or miseducated and also vested interests groups. These people place narrow and parochial loyalties such as those towards caste, language, religion, region, etc. Another problem posed by culture lag is that of mal-adjustment which manifests itself in the form of fissiparous or separatist tendencies, nativism (praising one's past glories), resistance to social change, non-adaptive behaviours, etc. How to solve the problems posed by culture lag is a very significant question. What can educators do about it. Here are a few answers that have been provided to this question :

(*a*) Provide high quality free, compulsory and universal education. This is a basic condition to organise further programmes of national integration.

(*b*) Provide non-formal education : education or re-education of the non-enrolled, drop-outs and adult population.

(*c*) Provide equal opportunities in education for the backward classes. Provision of special facilities such as reservation of seats, award of stipends and scholarships, hostel facilities, etc.

Through the programmes of compulsory and non-formal education, promote inter-cultural understanding among the different sub-cultures of the nation. Inter-cultural understanding implies an understanding of the cultural diversities among the sub-cultures of India and an honest appreciation of the highlighting features of these diversities. For instance, there are different systems of music practised and propagated in different parts of India such as the Hindustani, Karnatak, Ravindra sangeeth, Qawwali, etc. An expert or lover of one system must try to understand and appreciate the other forms also; he may not be expected to learn the other systems equally well. Similarly there are five recognised schools of dancing such as the Bharathanatyam, Kathakkali, Kathak, Manipuri and Odissi. The lover of one form should not be prejudiced against the others. Such an attitude should be applied to other diversities such as food habits, dress, folkways, language, etc. Hence inter-cultural understanding (also called as cross-cultural understanding) discourages extreme sentimental attachment to the heritage of one's own sub-culture to the utter disregard of other sub-cultures. Emphasising the importance of inter-cultural understanding Dr. N. V. Thirtha says : "India is a heterogeneous society with different sub-cultures.

The Indian Constitution has even guaranteed the right for each sub-culture to conserve and promote their own unique cultures. Therefore, under the present conditions of democratic pluralism, the only alternative to national unity is to bring about inter-cultural understanding among the different sub-cultures of the nation."[9] It is through inter-cultural education that inter-cultural understanding can be brought about. Inter-cultural education is that education which has been designed with a view to promote understanding and appreciation of cultural diversities. Inter-cultural education must be provided within the framework of the Indian Constitution which stands for secularism, socialism and democracy and guarantees, justice, liberty, equality and fraternity.

Objectives of Education for National Integration

(*a*) to bring about a correct understanding and appreciation of cultural diversities among the different sub-cultures;

(*b*) to develop a commitment—both mental and behavioural to the ideals of democracy as set out in the Constitution;

(*c*) to develop healthy appreciation of one's sub-culture therein avoiding bias against other sub-cultures.

The above are some of the more significant objectives of education for national integration.

School Programmes

There are many things that the scnool can do to promote

national integration. The programmes of the school must be phased. In the first phase children must be made aware of the existence of and the similarities and diversities in the different sub-cultures. This is at the early stages of schooling. This phase is basic to the subsequent phases. At the second phase opportunities must be provided for children to discuss common problems with objectivity and concern. At the third and final stage, that is by the end of the schooling period, children must be provided opportunities through work-situations to work for common goals and interests. Both attitudinal and behavioural changes must be brought about by school programmes.

Curriculum For National Integration

There are two views in regard to the nature of curriculum organisation for national integration. One opinion is that a special area on inter-sub-cultural variations must be included in the existing curriculum. But this may not be a practicable suggestion in view of the competing claims of different objectives of education. It is difficult to accommodate all the claims. Another opinion is that an orientation towards national integration should be provided in the existing curriculum, wherever it is possible. It must become an integral part of the curriculum, both curricular and co-curricular.

Text Books

A word of caution is necessary in analysing or writing textbooks so as to promote national integration. Words with emotional overtones must be used to highlight the significant and distinguishing features of one's own sub-culture without developing prejudices against other sub-cultures. Omission of facts, prejudiced statements and sweeping generalisations must be avoided.

Methods of Teaching

The problem-solving and project methods of teaching lend abundant scope for promoting national integration. Group discussions also have a place.

REFERENCES

1. "India : Its Administration and progress."
2. "Oxford History of India", Oxford University Press, London, 1906.
3. "Democratic philosophy of Education", Kitab Mahal, Allahabad, 1966, p. 20.
4. Quoted after Dr. Rajendra Prasad : "India Divided", Hind Kitab Ltd., 1947, Bombay, p. 9.
5. "The National Culture of India", Jaico, Bombay, 195 , p. xvi.
6. "National Integration". Jullundur University, 1964, p. 38.
7. "Comparative Education", R and K Paul, London, 1958, (III Ed.), p. 38.
8. "Discovery of India", Meridian Books, London, 1956, p. -9.
9. "National Integration", *op. cit.*, p. 117.

CHAPTER 13

Education for International Understanding

The urge of man to bring about understanding between and among nations is not new. Even as early as 500 BC, the Stoics of Greece expressed themselves in favour of it in their advocacy of 'Cosmopolitanism'. But for the first time in recent history Jeremy Bentham coined the word 'internationalism' which is currently referred to as international understanding. In simple terms, international understanding is an understanding of the problems of mankind and their relation to us. Such an understanding is characterised by an attitude of mind as follows[1] :

(*a*) A desire to live together with all persons within a

social framework that provides equal justice for all without considering their nationality, class, race, colour, creed or status. Equal justice is not identical justice; it is not necessary that the social framework be the same everywhere. The UNO is an illustration of such a desire.

(*b*) An attempt to encourage and enable all people to plan co-operatively and work together constructively. The United Nations Commission on Trade and Development (UNCTAD) is an in illustration of such an attempt.

Nationalism and Internationalism

Internationalism should not be confused as anti-nationalism or nationalism as anti-internationalism. In fact internationalism is impossible without healthy nationalism. If the sentiments and love of man are considered in the form of a pyramid then self-love (self-respect) and love of his home may be taken to form the base and love of internationalism as the apex with successive intermittent stages of love of sub-group (kins), group (clas s, caste, race, etc.), village, town, District, State and Nation. One who is guided by the principles of universal love, compassion, justice, equality and fraternity does not experience any conflict between national and international interests or in between any successive stages. But if nationalism means 'My Country, right or wrong' then such an attitude is neither sound nor healthy. One must love one's country and support it only when it is just. For example a father may love his child, but he may not keep quiet when it beats other children without provocation or snatches away something from them or engage in similar actions. He should not encourage the child while he plays mischiefs that are harmful to others.

The following example may illustrate how nationalism is not anti-internationalism. When a father says he loves his child, he does not mean that he hates children of other parents. Similarly when a father says that he loves all children he does not need to hate his own child. Much depends on the discriminative interpretation of the concepts of nationalism and inter nationalism. As such there is inherently no contradiction between the two. Dr. Walter H.C. Lewis, formerly Deputy-Director General of UNESCO has brought out the relation between nationalism and internationalism in his description of the meaning of international understanding : "It is an attempt to promote a comprehension of the ways of life, the values, and aspirations of all peoples of the world. It is an attempt to understand the requirements of living together on this planet. In this sense 'understanding' includes the necessity of comprehending our own ways of living, as well as the ways of other people. In short, international understanding is the ability to critically and objectively observe and appraise the conduct of men everywhere to each other, irrespective of the nationality or culture to which they may belong. To do this one must be able to detach oneself from one's own particular cultural and national prejudices and to observe men of all nationalities, cultures and races as equally important varieties of human beings inhabiting this earth."[2] Essentially international understanding implies an acceptance of the rights of all nations for an honourable existence. It implies an obligation to create conditions in which relations between different nations would be regulated and disputes, if any, settled not by force but through negotiations, discussions and compromise.

Needs for Developing International Under-standing

The needs for developing international understanding are numerous and diverse. But four needs may be considered as significant.

(a) *Progress of Human Civilisation* : There has been tremendous progress in all spheres of life; from paleolithic and neolithic ages man has progressed to the nuclear and space age, from cow-dung and bullock-cart to computer technology, from dictatorship to communism and democracy, from aristocracy to Republican forms of Government, in values and beliefs from Adam and Eve to origin of species, from slave trade to equality and tyranny to liberty. Similarly there has been progress in mathematics, medicine, agriculture, oceanography, metallurgy and all walks of life.

Progress in human civilisation has not been achieved by any race, caste, class, ethnic or national group but people working in different corners of the world and belonging to diverse groups have achieved it. This progress has been shared by all the people of the world. The present state of the world is due to the combined, cumulative and patient efforts of many nationals.

(b) *Synchronisation of Cultures* : International trade and modern means of transport have given rise to a continuous interaction between and among all the people of the world. The world of man is enlarging though the world is shrinking. Today there is no pure (cent per cent) American, Indian or Englishman. That is why Bernard Shaw had funnily remarked; "A cent per cent American (original, native, Red Indian) is ninetynine per cent a fool." Both the East and the West have influenced each other. For instance, the ideas of liberty, equality and fraternity which were consciously felt during the French revolution have pervaded the whole world. Ideas of Charles Darwin, Karl Marx, Sigmund Freud and a score of other great men have influenced the thinking world. Now needs and problems of humanity are similar : the cure for dreadful diseases, population problems, pollution, nuclear non-prolifira-tion, etc.

When two persons from different countries meet each other for trade or other economic purposes they also unintentionally become familiar with and in many cases influenced by each others, culture. There has been a diffusion of cultures. The world has become a melting pot of all cultures.

(c) *Interdependence of Nations* : Every country may try to be self-reliant but no country can be self-sufficient. All the countries of the world depend upon each other either for their consumer goods or for raw materials; in certain cases even for finished non-consumable goods. There have been so many agencies such as CEATO. CENTO. ECM, SAARC, etc. symbolising this inter-dependence. The state of inter-dependence through international trade is such that a trade-pact of say Japan with another country say Mexico affects the price of consumer goods or raw materials in other parts of the world. No country can remain free from any tilt in the international economic balance. As Prof K.G. Saiyidin puts it : "A war starts in Europe and three million people find themselves uprooted from their homeland, cut off from their national occupation and deprived of all that makes life pleasant, gracious and meaningful."[3] Not only there is dependence on goods and services but also on technical know-how. In recent years there has been observed a dependence in cultural life. The value-system of one nation initiates changes in the value-system of another nation. As if acutely sensing the need for interdependence among nations Nehru made the opening statement in his speech at the Geneva Peace Conference thus : "The choice before the world today is peaceful co-existence or no-existence at all."[4]

The needs discussed so far for international understanding have a positive overtone. There is also a rather negative reason to realise this objective.

(*d*) *Threat of a Nuclear War* : A nuclear war means one mass of total annihilation. It implies a colossal calamity at one stroke of accumulated civilisation. The progress in sophisticated nuclear war technology has been so enarmous that it is very dangerous to take risks about that. To balance this progress a commitment to international peace and understanding is very essential. The threat of a nuclear war is haunting every nation and especially those who are ignorant of nuclear war technology. John F. Kennedy the former President of the United States had said in 1962 in his first presidential address that : "We should abolish the weapons of war before they abolish us." There is a need for the nuclear nations to guarantee the non-proliferation of nuclear weapons and the security of non-nuclear nations.

Barriers for International Understanding

There are many problems which pose obstacles and barriers in the progress of man towards international understanding. Some of these problems are referred to here—

(*a*) *Secrecy* about the nuclear strength of nations.

(*b*) *Racial prejudices* : One of the strongest barriers in the way towards international understanding. H.G. Wells had suggested interracial marriage as the solution for all the problems of the world.

(*c*) *Inequality of Countries* : in size, resources, growth rates national income, scientific and technological progress, etc. Inequality has led to a sort of inferiority complex among less developed nations and consequently to corresponding prejudices and preferences.

(*d*) *Lack of National Solidarity* : When the people of many countries do not cherish a feeling that they are nationals of a nation and instead owe their loyalties to parochial groups and ideas, are victims of regionalism, communalism, casteism, etc., how can they be expected to look at the world as an organisation of brothers and equals. So, national integration and a sense of national solidarity are a prerequisite for international understanding.

Objectives of Education for International Understanding

The following specific objectives would serve to realise the general objective (or aim) of education for international understanding.

(*a*) highlight the peaceful uses of atomic energy and vividly picturise (describe) the devastating consequences of the misuse of nuclear energy. For instance the uses of an atomic reactor for constructive purposes and the misuse of atomic bomb for destructive designs may be discussed in a comparative frame ;

(*b*) give a basic knowledge of the life and culture of different nations of the world ;

(*c*) develop a spirit of tolerance (not indifference) towards the ways of life of different people of the world—their religion, customs and traditions, dress and food habits, etc ;

(*d*) develop rational thinking about the problems of other nations, inter-nation problems and their relevance to the nation to which the children belong ;

(*e*) develop a sympathetic attitude towards the (problems of the) less developed nations of the world; in general a concern for the welfare of humanity ;

(*f*) develop a willingness to place common good before personal interests ;

(*g*) strengthen the sense of national solidarity ;

(*h*) inculcate a belief in the ideals like fraternity,[5] equality, liberty and justice ;

Role of Schools :

If the objectives stated above are defined conceretely in terms of the role of the school, then it may read as follows. However, the list is not exhaustive. The role of the school depicted here refers only to co-curricular dimension, not the curricular subjects—

(*a*) Provide information about other countries; their problems and their contribution to the progress of human civilisation; their role in international economic, social, political and cultural spheres of life.

(*b*) Provide information about the UNO and its various agencies; about the *raison de etre*, purposes, structure and achievements of the UNO. There are three approaches to do this—(*i*) the historical approach, where the history of the UNO and other agencies are traced, (*ii*) the problem approach where discussion about the role of UNO or any of its agencies in the solution of international economic or political problems would take place, (*iii*) the project approach where children learn about UNO and its wings through the use of project method of learning.

(*c*) Arrange model UNO in the school.

(*d*) Arrange exhibitions displaying the achievements of the UNO.

(*e*) Observe red-letter days of universal significance such as the UNO or the Red-cross day.

(*f*) Observe the birth anniversary of great persons of the world.

(*g*) Arrange debates, seminars, symposiums and special talks on topics of international interest.

(*h*) Show films on different countries; their cultural differences.

(*i*) Encourage children to go and collect funds for international causes; for instance red-cross and UNICEF.

Curriculum and Methods of Teaching

There is no need for a separate curriculum to develop international understanding. The existing subjects of the curriculum lend themselves to such a treatment. For instance while teaching History it is essential to teach about the way human culture has developed rather than about kings, their wars and wives. It is desirable to impress upon the common heritage of mankind—a fruit of untold turmoils, trials and tribulations, labours and sufferings of countless millions and unrecognised martyrs of the world. To illustrate, some years ago, the text book on world history prescribed for high schools, was titled as 'Struggle of Modern Man'. Similarly geography must be taught as the adjustment of man to his physical environment and the various types of adjustment of man to his differing geographical environment must be highlighted. The humanistic spirit must be brought out while teaching literature. Science and technology must be taught as an achievement of the combined efforts of scientists from different parts of the world. The universality of symbols, concepts and vocabulary of mathematics as a language of science must be highlighted. However, much depends upon the way these subjects are handled that the effect would be brought about.

Role of the Teacher

The role of the teacher set to develop international understanding is highly delicate. He is expected to rouse the patriotic spirit in children and at the same time develop an attitude of looking far beyond the nation and identifying one's interests and the interests of one's nation with the interests of those living far beyond the frontiers of one's own nation. Here follows a suggestive list of expectations from the teacher.

(*a*) He should have a world-perspective : a knowledge of the culture of the whole world. He must possess a quality of imagination to foresee the consequences of the policies of his nation on other nations and *vice versa*.

(*b*) He should have a tolerant attitude. The teacher should be able to appreciate the cultural diversities of other people and also sympathise with their problems.

(*c*) He must be free from prejudices and biases. He needs to be receptive to truth and objective in thinking. The teacher should possess an open mind and clear thinking.

(*d*) He should basically be a lover of peace and co-operation.

The role of the teacher in bringing about I.U. has been very well described by L.S. Kensworthy. Though it is long, still it would be useful to quote it in full : "The teacher should be an integrated individual, skilled in the art and science of human relations and conscious of the wide variety of behaviour pattern in the world to which he may have to adjust. He is rooted in his own family, country and culture, but able to identify himself with the people of other countries and cultures. He is informed about the contemporary world scene and its historical background and concerned about improving the conditions of people every where. Moreover he is an intelligent participant in efforts to improve his own community and nation, mindful of their relationships to the world community, clear in his own mind as to the goals of education for international understanding, conversant with methods and resources for such programme and able to help create world-minded children and youth, but stressed by a dynamic faith or philosophy of life whose basic tenets can be universalised."[6]

Conclusion

Human civilisation will be at stakes if the cherished goal

of international understanding turns out to be an utopia. Moreover the hall-mark of a progressive human civilisation is an increasing belief in the value of peaceful co-existence. The faith of UNESCO symbolises this cherished goal. The preamble of the UNESCO runs thus : "Since wars begins in the minds of men, it is in the minds of men that the defences of peace must be constructed—the wide diffusion of culture and education of humanity for justice, liberty and peace are indispensable to the dignity of man and constitute a sacred duty which all the nations must fulfil in a spirit of mutual assistance and concern."[7]

The 'defences of peace' referred to above by the UNESCO must be constructed in the minds of men when they will be students in schools and colleges. The Kothari Commission on education had said that "The destiny of India is being shaped in her classrooms."[8] If this statement is not an exaggeration, then it can easily be said that not only that of India, but "The density of mankind (the world). is being shaped in her classrooms."

REFERENCE

1. Connell, W.F. : Readings in the Foundations of Education,
2. "Education and International life."
3. "Education for International Understanding."
4. Speeches of Nehru.
5. There is a story of a youth carrying a child on his back to the top of a hill. A passerby smiled at him and asked : "The steps to the hill are steep and the sun is scorching. Don't you feel the

burden." Then the youth replted : "That sir is not a burden. He is my younger brother." This must be the attitude of more developed nations towards less developed nations.

6. Bulletin of the National Association of Secondary School Principals, USA.

7. Preamble of UNESCO, UNESCO Charter Document.

8. 1966, p. 1.

CHAPTER 14

Curriculum

The key elements in the evaluation of an educational system centre around three important questions. They are the "Why ?" "What ?" and "How ?" of education. Why is education being given ? In other words, what are the objectives of education ? Then, what is being taught so as to realise these objectives. This question refers to the content of instruction. The third question refers to the methods of teaching and is posed as how is the instruction being given ? The second question refers to the curriculum. The analysis of the concepts, principles and forms of curriculum is an important area of educational theory.

The word curriculum is from the Latin root 'curricere' which originally meant a 'course', usually a 'race-course'. The word course is to be noted because much of the popular reference to curriculum is in terms of 'course of studies', though there is a difference between the two. Curriculum is a comprehensive term and includes in its fold a course of studies. As Gwynn brings out the relation between the two : "curricumlum may be defined as all the experience which pupils have while under the direction of the school ; thus defined, it includes both classroom and extra-classroom activities.........courses of study may be defined as that part of the curriculum which is organised for classroom use. They suggest content, procedures, aids and materials for the use and guidance of teachers, pupils and administrators. Thus considered, they contain only part of the individual pupil's curriculum."[1]

Curriculum refers to both organised and informal activities of school life. School life need not imply life of the child within the four walls of the school alone, but extends beyond that. Curriculum is co-terminous with the life of the pupil. As Dewey would say: "The child and the curriculum are simply two ends of a continuum-life."[2] The definition of the curriculum assumed by the Secondary Education Commission of which Dr. A L Mudaliar was Chairman is of relevance to the discussion and is quite comprehensive : "Curriculum includes the totality of experiences that a pupil receives through the manifold activities that go on in the school, in the class-room, library, laboratory, workshop, playgrounds, and in the numerous informal contacts between teachers and pupils. In this sense the whole life of the school becomes the curriculum which can touch the life of the students at all points and help in the evolution of a balanced personality."[3] Acceptance of such an all-embracing definition as this would warrant a deeper and manifold attention to the life of the child inside as well as outside the school than is usually devoted to it. As such the ethos and traditions that the school develops and maintains over the years can also be conceived of as part of the curriculum. Even a cursory glance at many of the shed-like recognised teaching shops that proliferate in sophisticated urban conglemorations and have a growth potential equal to that of mushrooms leaves one wondering whether such definition of the curriculum as referred to above tend to overshoot the mark of reality. But things are what they are, and definitions are what they ought to be.

Curriculum is only a means to an end. If aims of education are taken to be the ends, then curriculum is the means through which the ends are attempted to be realised. A similar conception of the curriculum in a metaphorical sense has been given by Prof. Cunningham : "Curriculum is a tool in the hands of an artist (educator) to mould his material (educand) in accordance with his ideals in his studio (school)." Though his definition is impressive, still the usage of the word 'mould' in the treatment of children is objectionable. The child is not like lifeless matter that lends itself to be moulded. They are responsive and reactive. They have their own individuality. The one-sided psychology of John Locke and Watson that the child is pliable like plastic is outdated. As such curriculum has to cater to the individualities of children.

Curriculum in the Educative Process

The place and importance of the curriculum in the educative process needs no overemphasis. The general aims of education receive concrete expression through the curriculum. It translates ideals into action. It is the crucial link between objectives and outcomes. As King and Brownell write : "*Deliberately designed activity of life is education*, deliberately designed portion of education is schooling, the heart of schooling is curriculum,......"[4] Putting the idea from another angle, aims of life determine the aims of education which in turn determine the aims of schooling. These are in turn defined in terms of

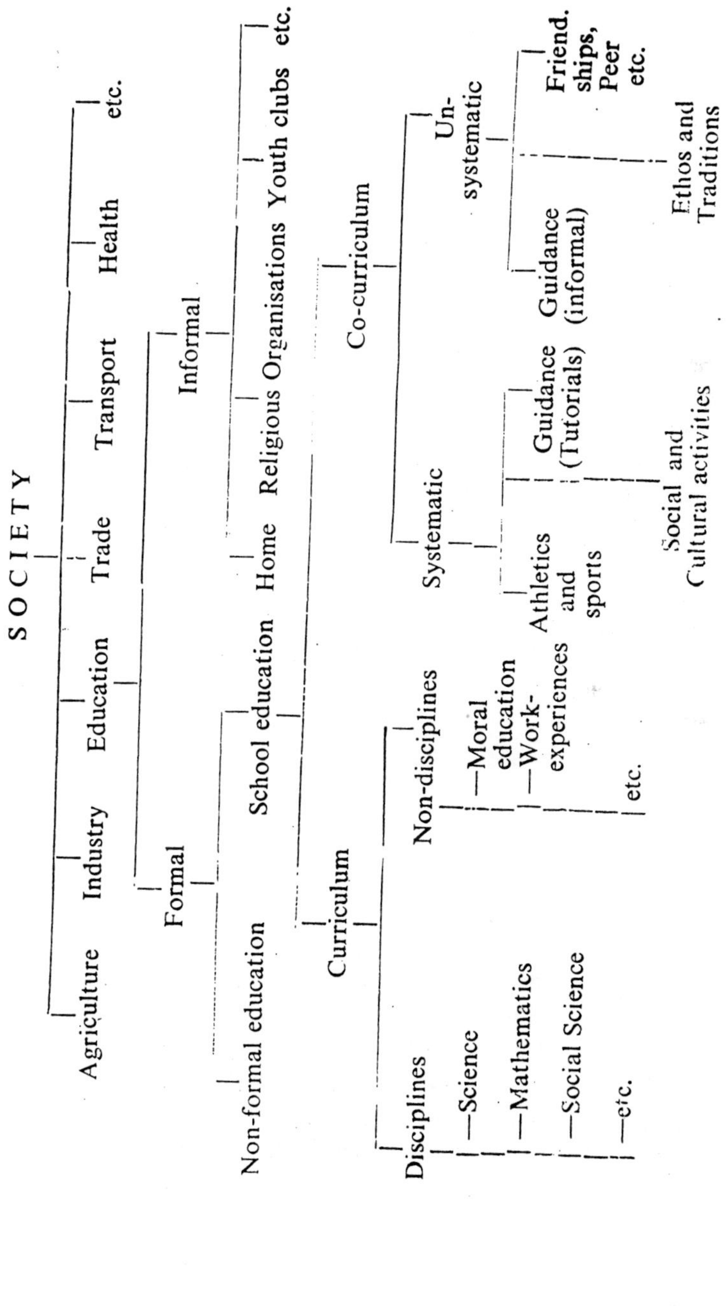
SOCIETY
Agriculture
Industry
Education
Trade
Transport
Health
etc.
Formal
Informal
Non-formal education
School education
Home
Religious Organisations
Youth clubs
etc.
Curriculum
Co-curriculum
Disciplines
—Science
—Mathematics
—Social Science
—etc.
Non-disciplines
—Moral education
—Work-experiences
etc.
Systematic
Un-systematic
Athletics and sports
Guidance (Tutorials)
Guidance (informal)
Friend. ships, Peer etc.
Social and Cultural activities
Ethos and Traditions

objectives of teaching school subjects and other school programmes. As such aims of life are realised through curriculum. Here follows an analytic and diagrammatic representation of the place of curriculum in the life of a society.

If society is conceived of as a 'system' education is a sub-system which inter-acts with other sub-systems such as agriculture, industry, health, trade, transport, banking, communications, etc. Curriculum should be able to reflect the interdependence of education with other sub-systems.

Principles of Curriculum Construction

There are a few basic principles that need to be kept in view while designing a curriculum or evaluating it. They are discussed here.

(*a*) Keep the aims of education in view—one of the few around which the curriculum has to evolve is the aims of individual and social life. Curriculum has to reflect the life, needs and aspirations of the people. These will be defined in the form of aims of education. As is well known, if philosophy gives a design for living, education is an attempt to realise that way of life. As such knowledge of educational philosophy is essential for curriculum construction.

(*b*) Keep the child's needs, interests and capabilities in view. It is universally accepted that children differ in their abilities, interests, needs, aptitudes and aspirations. They also differ in their 'life-space'[5], their experiences, their perception of the surrounding universe and ability to profit from experiences. Therefore, curriculum should be based upon a knowledge of individual differences among children. A study of educational psychology and specially developmental psychology would be useful in this direction.

(*c*) Keep the needs of the immediate community in view : A curriculum should enable the pupils to function in later life as successful and efficient members of the community. It has to be realistic. Students should not feel alienated from their own surroundings. The curriculum for a predominantly agricultural community ought to be different in certain ways from one that is an industrial or mining community. Similarly the curriculum for a fisherman's or shipping or banking or trading community has to be distinctive in certain respects. In other words the means of production of a community has to partly determine the structure of curriculum.

From another point of view, of the state of social dynamics, curriculum has to be community—based. The curriculum for a conservative, orthodox, superstitious, developing community has to be different from that for a creative, forward-looking, dynamic and progressive community................................ A knowledge of educational sociology would be quite useful for the purpose.

(*d*) Keep the utility in view—How far the curriculum would be useful for the individual and the society is an important question to be posed while constructing a curriculum. Curriculum must be able to equip the individual to sell himself in the employment market. The necessary skills and attitudes for a gainful employment must be a criterion for curriculum construction. This refers to the vocationalisation of school education. The issue of vocationalisation of school education is sufficiently controvertial. Higher education too, save the professional courses is rather liberal in nature than vocational. Instances like science graduates working as clerks and commerce graduates as social welfare workers are not few and far between. A study of economics of education would be useful in making and guarding the utility of the curriculum. Cost-benefit and rates of return studies would be of immense use in constructing, discarding or modifying a curriculum.

There are a few minor principles of curriculum construction. They are : the principles of integration or fusion of the different subjects of the curriculum, principles of flexibility or elasticity and variety to cater to the varying needs of students with different intellectual equipment, social and economic backgrounds, geographical regions, etc. The curriculum should also provide for the pursuit of healthy leisure-time activities.

Subject *versus* Experience Centred Controversy in Organisation

The traditional curriculum is an organisation of different subjects such as physics, chemistry, biology, history, geography, mathematics and the languages. It is sequentially arranged and the child has to cover it stage by stage. Knowledge is logically segmented, compartmentalised and fed to the child. The completion of the first stage is essential for the completion of the second stage and the process continues till the end.

There was a strong reaction to this kind of organisation in the twentieth century by many educational thinkers like John Dewey, Kilpatrick and others. According to them, acquisition of knowledge is not the chief end with which a child has to pursue a curriculum. It is always incidental to the acquisition of skills, attitudes, interests and experiences of life. The organisation of the curriculum should not be determied by the internal logic of the subject matter but by the level of maturation, rhythms of growth and development, previous experiences, personality patterns, interests and abilities of comprehension of children and the community setting.

As such there is a controversy in the field of curriculum organisation. The controversy can be posed in the form of these questions : should the organisation of the curriculum be logical or psychological, prescriptive or elective, preparing for life or providing life, adult-centred or child-centred, in brief, subject-centred or experience-centred ?

Arguments in Favour of Subject-Centred Curriculum

Children understand concepts and processes better and easily when they are presented to them in a systematic way. For instance, it is necessary, for them to understand what is 'burning' before they are told about a burning candle. It is easier to understand an organised material than to receive matter, organise it and then understand it. As an illustration, study the following sets of words :

(*a*) Ram, Morning, Coffee. Bath, School, Friend, Quarrel, Head Master, Punishment ;

(*b*) Ram, Head Master, Bath, Punishment, Coffee, Friend, Morning, Quarrel, School.

It is easier to derive a meaning out of the first set of words than the second, because an experience is presented in an organised way. Also, it is possible to define the content and scope of the curriculum. Once the boundary is defined, then text-books can be written that will cover the syllabus. Further a standardised scheme of evaluation can be followed.

Criticism

However, the criticism against the subject-centred curriculum is that it is more logical than psychological, hence, unsound. As Dewey says : "Classification is not a matter of child experience: things do not come to the child in a pigeon-holed way."[6] Further, the subject-centred curriculum is said to be remote from the democratic values that the school seeks to realise.[7] Values such as creativity, cooperation, social concern, reflective thinking, tolerance etc., cannot be developed through subject-centred curriculum. Being an organised curriculum imposed on children, it can develop only authoritarian values.

Arguments in Favour of Experience-Centred Curriculum

The experience centred curriculum is very closely related to the life, needs, problems and interests of children. It utilises to the maximum degree the physical resources and the social and political life of the community. Thus, it has an advantage in unifying the school with the community. Learning process is to be set in a democratic way under this curricular organisation. As such it is easier to inculcate democratic values. Most of all, it is based on the new psychology of learning wherein the child is the focus of all activities.

Criticism

Those who are critical of the experience-centred curriculum doubt whether children are able to deduce generalisations on the basis of their experience. They feel that children will get themselves lost in the woods counting the trees and fail to get a broad, organised perspective of life. Further, it is rather difficult to evaluate the outcomes of learning through this curricular organisation.

Conclusion

The values of the subject-centred and experience-centred curriculum should be harmoniously integrated. The values of direct experience should be combined with those of systematic organisation. For instance, direct experiences should be provided for in a subject-centred curriculum or organisation of experiences should be brought about and generalisations arrived at in an experience-centred curriculum.

Prof. Hirst has advocated the integration of the curriculum. This has to be achieved in two ways : "a formal structure has to be achieved within different forms of knowledge ; again these structured components of knowledge should be linked together in formal ways. Different forms of knowledge should be provided systematically but integrated under certain specified general themes."[8]

Defects of the Existing Pattern of Curriculum

Of all the deficiencies of the educational system in India one defect that clearly stands out is related to the "Curriculum." In fact a number of other defects in the educational system are the result of defective curriculum. The improvement of the C^m is the burning topic of the day throughout the world and the gravity of the problem is pronounced in developing countries like India. As the *Kothari Commission Report* says "The school C^m is in a state of flux all over the world today. In developing countries it is generally criticised for not meeting the needs of modern times. Some of the glaring shortcomings of the present-day C^m are :

1. *Very Conception of the C^m is Norrow* : C^m is thought of as that portion of knowledge and experience by acquiring a

moderate mastery of which one can get an admission to the higher stages.

Primary School C^m : For instance the mastery of it is considered as a passport to the secondary school. Similarly the mastery of the *Secondary School C^m* is considered as the passport to the institutions of higher learning ; curriculum experts often lose sight of the ends which the C^m serves: Education, according to the modern conception, should not be delimited to acquisition of knowledge but extended to the development of values. But the present C^m lays a lot of premium on knowledge. As the *Kothari Commission* (p. 184) Report says : Against the background of the striking curricular developments that are taking place abroad, the school C^m in India will be found to be very narrowly conceived and largely out-of-date.

2. *It is Bookish and Theoretical* : The C^m is full of bookish knowledge and there is no scope for practical activities and as such conceptualisation of learning is far from possible. As a result, our schools have become knowledge—shops and pupils knowledge—mongers. As the Kothari Commission says : "Our schools are mostly concerned with the imparting of knowledge. The C^m places a premium on bookish knowledge and rote learning, makes inadequate provision for practical activities and experiences."

3. *It is Out of Tune with Life* : It takes little note of the challenging day-to-day economic, social and political issues that confront children in later life (when they become citizens) and very poorly reflects them in the classroom. As Kothari Commission writes : "The development of useful skills and the inculcation of the right kind of interests, attitudes and values needs sufficient emphasis. Therefore, the C^m becomes

not only out of step with modern knowledge, but also out of tune with the life of the people."

4. *The C^m is Highly Departmentalised* : The C^m is overcrowded with too many subjects and the relationship between and among the subjects is far from satisfactory. Such compartmentalisation does not help the pupils to think coherently. There is no correlation or fusion or integration of subjects.

5. *It is not Flexible* : It does not cater to the diverse tastes and talents of children effectively.

6. *Segmentation of School Life* : It demands the teachers to cover the portions of information in set class periods which discourages them to be enthusiastic about practical activities. A day in the school is so segmented that teachers are not left with sufficient time to make use of field-trips, moving pictures, plays or such other constructive activities which vitalise learning.

7. *It is Dominated by Examinations* : The public examination and other class examinations have such an impact upon the teachers and pupils that teachers are more concerned about getting larger percentage of passes and get pats on their back ; on the other hand students are concerned about securing more marks in the examination through which they can get a number of benefits like admission to institutions of higher learning or award of free-studentships. Even the *Kothari Commission* (p. 185) refers to this aspect of the curricular deficiency.

9. *It is Partly Outmoded* : There are a good many information in the C^m which are not in tune with the realities of time. As the *Kothari Commission* (p. 184) refers to it there has been tremendous explosion of knowledge in recent years and

also a reformulation of the basic concepts in the physical, biological and social sciences. These changes are inadequately reflected in the existing school programmes. (Up-to-date information is not provided for children).

Remedies Suggested for the Improvement of the C^m : The C^m constructors should keep in view all the defects of the existing C^m that have been discussed so far. *Further* :

(*a*) C^m should be related to available facilities : C^m should be related to the quality of teachers, facilities available in the school, needs of the pupils with references to their socio-economic background etc; (Kothari Commission, p. 184.)

It is impossible to bring out such a relation with a rigid, State-wide C^m. Therefore,

(*b*) School should be given autonomy, within a broad framework, to devise, evolve and adopt curricula suited to their own needs. (Kothari Commission, p. 184.)

(*c*) Schools should be given freedom to experiment with new curricula.

(*d*) Formation of subject Teacher's Associations which can discuss about specific aspects of the C^m clearly and at a depth level, needs to be done. The NCERT can coordinate the work of these associations.

(*e*) Science should be a basic component of the C^m at all stages of school education.

(*f*) Work-experience should be an integral part of general education.

(*g*) At the secondary school level, vocationalisation of the C^m should be done *i.e.*, a vocational bias should be given to the C^m.

(*h*) Some kind of education in morals should be made compulsory for all the children. As Kothari Commission says : "A serious defect in the school C^m is the absence of provision for education in social, moral and spiritual values"......................... "We recommend, therefore, that conscious and organised attempts be made for imparting education in social, moral and spiritual values."

REFERENCES

1. Gwynn, J. Minor : "Curriculum Principles and Social Trends" Macmillan, N.Y., 1948, p. 225.
2. Dewey, John : "The Child and the Curriculum," *op. cit.*, p. 11.
3. Secondary Education Commission Report, 1952, p. 85.
4. "The curriculum and the disciplines of knowledge", preface, John Wiley and Sons, N.Y., (1966).
5. The term is used in the sense in which Kurt Lewin has used it.
6. "The child and the curriculum," pp. 10-11.
7. Harold Alberty : "Reorganising the high school curriculum," Macmillan Co., N.Y., 1953, p. 126.
8. Paul H. Hirst : "Knowledge and the Curriculum," R & K Paul, London, 1974, p. 150.

CHAPTER 15

Educational Philosophy of Mahatma Gandhi

The Man and his Mission

A coverage of biograpical information and personal life of Gandhi has been deliberately left out. It is presumed to be integral to the education of Indian readers of this book. However, it is tempting to reproduce here the observation of Albert Einstein about Gandhi. Being aware of the life and achievements of Gandhi, Einstein observed that : "Generations to come will scarce believe that ever a man, in flesh and blood, walked upon this earth." He performed miracles in Indian socio-political life without any magic wand but with his mystical life, magical speeches and writings, human philosophy and winnowing personal qualities. He was a man with a mission : freedom for India—political, economic, social, intellectual and spiritual freedom ; freedom from exploitation, oppression, wants, hunger, poverty, ignorance, evil social practices, fatalism, etc. ; His economic institutions, educational experiments, political and social activities were directed to this end.

Gandhi's Philosophy of Life

Two words are fundamental in his philosophy of life : 'Truth' and 'Non-violence'. Discovery of truth is the ultimate goal of life and non-violence is the means to that end. Till 1931 he used to say 'God is Truth'. But thereafter he began to assert that "Truth is God". At one place he has said : "Denial of God we have known. Denial of Truth we have not known. The most ignorant among men also have some truth in them. We are sparks of truth."[1] Gandhi believed thus :

BRAHMA SATYAM. JAGAT SPURTHIHI.
SATYA SHODHANAM JANMAHA.

[Cosmic principles are the Truth. Universe around provides the inspiration. Purpose of life is to discover the truth.]

Gandhi believed that God is there in every human being—not in the temple, church, mosque, synagogue, monastery, viharas, gurudwaras, but in the temple of humanity. For realising Truth or God, he advocated service to humanity. You have to work for their economic freedom. Gandhi observed : "God has to appear as a loaf of bread to make his presence felt in India." He attempted at a total revolution in Indian society—economic, social, political and intellectual revolution. Non-violence should be the spearhead of such a revolution. It should be the method of attack. It should be a silent revolution without bloodshed and not a violent revolution as those of French revolution, Russian revolution, Chinese cultural revolution etc. Non-violence is not 'a shield of the coward, but the sword of the courageous.' Violence is a intensely emotional act, while non-violence is a rational virtue. The objective is achieved through discussion, negotiation, persuasion and not through aggression, attack, terrorism and dictation. Non-violence is the weapon for social service and through that the realisation of truth. It is resorted to with pleasure and not for any profit. Such service can have no meaning unless one takes pleasure in it. When it is done for show or for fear of public opinion, it stunts the man and crushes his spirit.

Service which is rendered without joy, helps neither the servant nor the served. But all the other possessions pale into nothingness before service which is rendered in spirit of joy. In fact, even before Gandhi came to India from South Africa, the Indian community there organised a public farewell reception and gave innumerable gifts and cash as a token of appreciation of his services to them. He collected all of them, created a trust for the welfare of poor Indians in South Africa and donated the gifts and cash to the trust. He believed that a public servant should not accept any gratification for his services. He used to say that "Love of fellowmen is my religion." His philosophy is also succinctly called as humanistic and practical idealism.

Gandhi's Interest in Education

Gandhi's interest in education was the outcome of a revolt against the defects of the then British system of education. The British system of education was purely literary in content. It neglected the vocational and aesthetic dimensions of education.

The prevailing system of primary education was practically of no use in after-school-life and therefore-was almost useless. It divorced the child from his physical and social surroundings. The medium of instruction was largely English. Mass education was not possible through English medium. Learning of English brought up a separate class of English educated Indian people who were known to be intellectual elite of the country but cut off from the social stream of Indian life. As Lord Macaulay stated in his 'Minutes', he "wanted a class of people Indian in blood and colour, but English in taste, in morals and intellect, in opinions, etc. ;" Even William Bentinck had preferred occidental to oriental education for the Indians. The Britishers had utter contempt for everything Indian. Macaulay had said that "A single shelf of a European library is worth all the native literature of India." Their prejudices were reflected in Indian education and the defects were glaring. Gandhi pointed out in 1921 (non-cooperation movement period) that the British system of education was defective in three important ways :

(*a*) It is based upon foreign culture to the almost entire exclusion of Indian culture.

(*b*) It ignores the culture of the heart and the hand and is confined simply to the culture of the head, and

(*c*) Real education is impossible through a foreign medium.

Gandhi observed[2] that ; "The greatest visible evil of the present educational method, in itself evidence of deeper defects, is that it has broken up the continuity of our existence. All sound education is meant to fit one generation to take up the burden of the previous and to keep up the life of the community without breach or disaster. The burden of social life is continuous and if at any stage one generation gets completely out of touch with the efforts of its predecessors or in any case gets ashamed of itself or its culture, it is lost."

Gandhi's Educational Experiments

Gandhi was highly pragmatic in his outlook. He believed that truth is that which bears out in testable situations. It should withstand experimentation and testing. Whatever idea is experimentally verifiable becomes true. In fact, the title of his autobiography is "My Experiments with Truth." Likewise, he tested all his educational ideas through experiments in education and then advocated them. His educational philosophy evolved through these experiments. His educational ideas did not suddenly emerge out of a vacuum. They are the outcomes of long years of his sustained thinking and experience of nearly 40 years both in South Africa and India.

He had been impressed by the ideas of John Ruskin ; "Unto the last." Three ideas struck him :

(*a*) Good of the individual is contained in the good of all,

(*b*) Dignity of labour has to be valued—a lawyer's work and a barber's work—both are dignified as the *ends* of both are to earn a livelihood and as their *means* are just.

(*c*) A life of labour is worth living—life of a tiller of the soil, handicraftsmen etc. ; His educational experiments were also guided by such thinking.

These ideas partly guided his experiments also.

South Africa

Durban, 1897. Gandhi did not send his children to European schools because of his disbelief in English medium education. He himself taught them through their mother-tongue, Gujarati.

Phoneix Settlement

South Africa, 1904. Gandhi started a school in South Africa with 30 children. Instruction was given both in literary aspects and training in agriculture and painting. It was an ideal school-workshop wherein both theory and practice were integrated.

Tolstoy Farm

Transvaal, 1911. This was an ashram set up with the help and guidance of Hermann Kallenbach, a German co-worker. People belonging to various religions—Hindus, Muslims, Parsis, Christians—lived together. Some Hindu girls were also there. More importance was given to culture of the heart and character building. Even physical culture was emphasised through cooking, scavenging and gardening. Learning was to be a joyous adventure and teachers were expected to set an example.

Shanthiniketan

Bengal 1914. Gandhi stayed with Rabindranath Tagore at his Shanthiniketan and with his group from South Africa.

Satyagraha Ashrama

Kochrab, Ahmedabad, May 1915. Training was given to the members to qualify themselves for service of the country. This service was to be consistent with universal welfare. This was an experiment in social education wherein people of different castes, creeds and religions lived there in terms of equality.

Sabarmathi Ashram : (1916)

The Satyagraha Ashram was shifted to Sabarmathi due to outbreak of plague in the former place. Sabarmathi had very good natural surroundings. Weaving was the principal activity here.

Champaran : (1917)

Gandhi attempted proper village education at Champaran. He opened six primary schools in six villages. The six villages were chosen on the condition that the villagers shall provide free board and lodging facilities to the teachers. The 3 R's, formal grammar, cleaniness and good manners were also taught to the children.

Wardha Scheme : (1937)

Gandhi launched a new scheme in 1937 to be applied on a nation-wide scale. It was earlier propounded in the columns of the 'Harijan'. It was a revolt against established orthodoxies in education. An All India Education Conference was held at Wardha on 22nd and 23rd October 1937. Ganhdi presided over this conference which was attended by Dr. Zakir Hussain, K.T. Shah, Vinoba Bhave, Mahadev Desai and Kaka Kalelkar. The following resolutions were passed :

(*a*) That in the opinion of this conference, free and compulsory education be provided for seven years on a nation-wide scale,

(*b*) That the medium of instruction be mother-tongue,

(*c*) Process of education to centre around a basic craft—manual and productive work—other subjects to be integrally related to this craft and the environment of the child,

(*d*) This system of education gradually to cover the remuneration of teachers.

Dr. Zakir Hussain worked out its syllabus by 2.12.1937. His report is known as Wardha Scheme on Basic National Education.

OUTSTANDING FEATURES OF THE WARDHA SCHEME

1. Free and compulsory education.

2. Education through craft—psychologically desirable—relieves the child from the tyranny of a purely academic and theoretical instruction ; it is socially desirable as it breaks down the status between manual and mental labour ; it is economical as teachers, remuneration is met through the production-gains of

the system. Here knowledge is related to life. It is concrete and real.

3. Educatlon is self-supporting. Considering the financial and political conditions of the country this was a welcome measure. It supports both the educative process and the child in later life.

4. Mother-tongue is the medium of instruction.

5. Ideal of citizenship is emphasised.

Basic Education in Practice

Dr. Zakir Hussain examined the scheme for the first time and placed his findings before the Indian National Congress at its Haripura Session in February 1938. This was approved with a slight difference of emphasis on the self-supporting aspect. The Central Advisory Board of Education made an enquiry into the working of basic education, under the chairmanship of B.G. Kher, in January 1939. The All India Education Board, known as Hindustani Talimi Sangh came into being at Segaon, Wardha, Madhya Pradesh in April 1939.

The first All India Basic Education Conference was held in December 1940 at Poona. It passed a resolution that English should not be taught for the first seven years of education except for those whose mother-tongue is English. The Second All India Basic Education Conference was held at Jumainagar in April 1941. It noted that the progress of Basic Education was slow due to the second world war. The Quit India Movement was launched on August 9, 1942. Gandhi was imprisoned and basic education receded to the background.

On his release he came out with a new vision of 'Nai Talim'—education for life and through life. Education was to be co-extensive with life ; the purpose was to lead a balanced and harmonious life. Cleanliness and health, citizenship, work and worship, play and recreation were organised in an integral way into a system of education. The All India Basic Education Conference was held at Sewagram in 1945. This was inaugrated by Gandhi and it assessed the progress of Basic Education in the preceding years as well as charted a plan of basic education, extending to four stages : Community orientation for basic education, pre-basic education, basic education and post-basic education. Even after independence, in April 1948, an All India Basic Education Conference was held at Bikram in Bihar which reiterated its faith in the efficacy of basic education.

Gandhi's Theory of Education

Gandhi's educational theory has four bases : (*a*) his educational experiments, (*b*) his general philosophy of life, (*c*) his dissatisfaction with the British legacy in education, and (*d*) his faith in education as an instrument of social, economic, political, moral and spiritual regeneration of India.

Meaning of Education

Gandhi believed in integrated education. He believed that the child had several innate potentialities which should be facilitated to blossom through the educational process. Physical, mental, social, emotional and spiritual development should be attempted through education. As he put it : "Education is drawing out of the best in child and man—body, mind and spirit." Education of the head, the heart and the hand should be pursued simultaneously. The British system catered only to the intellectual aspects—the head.

Gandhi observed[3] that : "I hold that true education of the intellect can come only through a proper exercise and training of the bodily organs, *e.g.*, : hands, feet, eyes, ears, nose, etc. In other words an intelligent use of the bodily organs in a child provides the best and quickest way of developing his intellect. But unless the development of the body and mind goes hand in hand with a corresponding awakening of the soul, the former alone would prove to be a poor lop-sided affair."

Gandhi also believed that education should transmit the cultural heritage and refine and enrich it for the benefit of posterity. However, education has to be life itself and through life.

Aims of Education

Gandhi's aims of education are both individual and social. He has tried to synthesise the two types of aims. Just like Plato who dreamt of an utopian, ideal State, similarly Gandhi dreamt of a 'Ramaraya'—a new social order based on Truth and Non-violence. He wanted to bring a total transformation in the life of the Indian society--economic, social, political and cultural life. Ramarajya also meant, vigilant, frank and fearless citizens and responsive government, just as in the story of the washerman in the epic novel Ramayana and the State's response to criticism.

Education, for the individual, is one that liberates. The motto of Gujarath Vidyapeeth, founded by Gandhi in 1920 is 'SA VIDYA YA VIMUKTAYA', education is that which liberates. "Liberation does mean spiritual liberation. It means freedom from all manner of servitude even in the present life."[4] He identified two forms of servitude—slavery to domination from outside, slavery to one's own natural impulses.

Character and citizenship are two other individual aims. Character is the end of knowledge. It includes all training useful for the service of humanity. It is rather engaging in good than restraining from evil. A sense of social responsibility is subsumed in the ideal of citizenship.

The most significant individual aim is the vocational aim. It is a utilitarian aim. Here, craft is the basis and centre of all education.

Gandhi and the Pupil

He believed that the child brings his own experiences to the school and they have to be reconstructed. Education is a process of 'drawing out' from the child. There is a lot of scope for the child to unfold its creative abilities and develop originality. He wanted the children to cultivate purity in thought, word and deed along with pursuit of knowledge.

Gandhi and Curriculum

Curriculum in Gandhi's scheme is activity-centred and craft-centred. As M. S. Patel has put it in style : "Craft occupies the position of the sun in the vast solar system of human life, satisfying our material needs in perfect harmony with the higher values of life."[5] The subjects in the curriculum included the following : (*a*) basic craft-agriculture, spinning, weaving etc., (*b*) mother-tonque, (*c*) mathematics—useful for craft and community-life, (*d*) social studies—social and economic life of the community, culture of the country, history of craft, etc ; (*e*) general science—nature study, zoology, physiology, hygiene, physical culture, anatomy, etc ; (*f*) drawing and music.

He advocated uniform education for boys and girls up to the fifth grade and diversified education thereafter—general science to be replaced by domestic science for girls along with craft for both. He laid special stress on development of good handwriting.

Gandhi, Teacher and Discipline

He wanted the teacher to be a 'model of behaviour', an 'image of society', 'a compendium of virtues'. He wanted teachers to teach by example than by precept. He opposed corporal punishment. How can an apostle of non-violence advocate anything like that ? He emphasised the value of self-discipline in life.

Gandhi and Textbooks

He believed that the true text-book for the pupils is their teacher. He did not want to load the student with innumerable textbooks.[6] He has observed :[7] "If I had my way, I would certainly destroy the majority of the present textbooks and encourage textbooks to be written which have a bearing on and correspondence with the home-life, so that a boy as he learns may react upon his immediate surroundings." Gandhi's views on textbooks are similar to that of Rousseau.

Gandhi and Methods of Teaching

Gandhi advocated the activity method—'learning by doing'. Method should be fused with matter, that is, education must revolve round vocational and manual activity at the centre, and all syllabi should be woven around vocational training. Education is through the medium of and in correlation with a productive work. He prefers oral instruction to personal study. "Children take in much more and with less labour through their ears than through their eyes."[8]

Gandhi and the School

The school should be an activity-school. It should be situated in a natural atmosphere. As M.S. Patel has observed : "The school of Gandhi's imagination will not be a place of passive absorption of information imparted second-hand, but will be a place of work, experimentation and discovery, because it will follow an activity—curriculum. The child acquires his knowledge actively and utilises it for the understanding and better control of his social environment."

Merits of Gandhi's System of Education

Several merits have been claimed or attributed to Gandhi's scheme. They are :

(*a*) It is a paido-centric education like those of Comenius, Rousseau, Pestalozzi and Montessori as it is based on child's needs and interests. It is highly psychological, being related to the child's immediate life. As Dr. Zakir Hussain committee observed : "Psychologically it is desirable, because, it relieves the child from the tyranny of a purely academic and theoretical instruction against which its active nature is making a healthy protest."

(*b*) There is no verbalism as it is based on an activity and is full of direct experiences. Vocational skills are promoted.

(*c*) Principle of Correlation : Craft is correlated with knowledge, life and environment. As the whole range of subjects are integrated round a productive activity, coordination and integration of knowledge is easy.

(*d*) Learning is easy as it is through mother-tongue as the medium of instruction.

(*e*) Co-education is there.

Demerits

Critiques of Gandhi's system of education have identified several limitations and defects. They are :

(*a*) Over-emphasis on economic aspects of the educative process. In actual implementation, teachers treated children as labourers and exhorted them to grow more vegetables or produce more clothes. Teachers' salaries and other monetary incentives were met through the labour of children. Hence, teachers gave undue attention to productive activity.

(*b*) Aesthetic dimension of life was neglected. Songs were limited to topics of takli and charka (spinning machine).

(*c*) Proper textbooks were not there.

(*d*) There was no organisation of subject matter.

(*e*) Initial investment on craft-material being heavy, necessity of expenditure on periodical repairs of equipment being there, it proved to be uneconomical.

(*f*) It was not in keeping with the modern scientific and technological developments. This is a very significant limitation.

(*g*) As the modernised and specialised employment market in science, engineering, technology, management, medicine and allied subjects etc ; demanded higher levels of education, students who came through a rural-oriented basic education were at a handicap. This situation would create a hiatus between craft-educated rural poor and modern-educated urban elites. The rural poor were discriminated through the educational structure itself. This would strengthen the already existing inequalities in society. It is unfair. It will be against the dream of a egalitarian society being envisaged in the country.

Gandhi's Scheme : An Assessment

One of the discussions that have surfaced in an assessment of Gandhi has centred round the question : Is Gandhi an idealist, a naturalist or a pragmatist educator ?

In his emphasis on an ideal society—a Ramarajya, he is an idealist. In his belief that education is for the liberation of the mind, it is for self-realisation through social service, his conception of the child as a spark of the divine etc ; he is an idealist. As he wrote in two issues of young India : "I believe in the absolute oneness of God (advaita) and therefore, of huminity. What though we may have many bodies ? We have but one soul. The rays of the sun are many through refraction. But they have the same source ?"[10] Again, "My creed is service of God, and therefore, of humanity."[11]

In his educational settings, in natural surroundings, Ashram—life, gurukula type of education etc ; he was a naturalist. His activity-centred curriculum also was in line with naturalistic sensory education. He was against text-book-education.

He was an experimentalist to the core, and hence a pragmatist. He believed in 'learning by doing' methods of teaching. He valued experience in life. He was always open-minded and did not claim any finality in truth. He practiced first and then preached it. In this sense, he was a pragmatist. As Dr. R. S. Mani has observed : "However, much his experiments may be characterised by qualities of accuracy, foresight and minuteness, he does not claim his results to be infalliable. Whatever appeared to be absolutely correct for him, seemed for the time being to be final."[12]

Winding up the discussion, M.S. Patel considers that Gandhi was three-in-one, an idealist, a naturalist and a pragmatist. As he puts it : "The real greatness of Gandhiji as an educationist consists in the fact that the dominant tendencies of naturalism, idealism and pragmatism are not separate and independent in his philosophy, but they are fused into a unity, giving rise to a theory of education which would suit the needs of the day and satisfy the loftiest aspirations of the human soul." This, and not the scheme of basic education is his greatest achievement.

Gandhi and Post-Independent Education in India

Interest in basic education waned, after Gandhi's death, for several reasons. The number of basic schools came down. But the message of Gandhi was clear and it tolled steadily against the over-academic nature of formal education. He had vehemently repeated the Clarion Call for according a status to work in the curriculum. His message was honoured by the Kothari Commission in its recommendation for work-experience in school education as an integral part of the curriculum. Advocating work-experience, the report observed that: "In our country, a revolutionary experiment was launched by Mahatma Gandhi in the form of basic education. The concept of work-experience is essentially similar. It may be described as a redefinition of his educational thinking in terms of a society launched on the road to industrialisation."[13] Even now it is accommodated in the form of socially useful productive work.

REFERENCES

1. Dr. S. Radhakrishnan (ed.): "Contemporary Readings in Indian Philosophy," Essay by Gandhi.
2. Gandhi : "Towards New Education," p. 26.
3. *Op. cit.* p. 42.
4. Gandhi : "To the Students" pp. 207, 288.
5. M.S. Patel : "Educational Philosophy of Mahatma Gandhi' Preface.
6. Gandhi : "My Experiments with Truth," pp. 411-412.

7. "Towards New Education" p. 29.
8. *op. cit.*, No. 6, p. 412.
9. Dr. Zakır Hussain : "Educational Reconstruction," p. 93.
10. "Young India" 25.9.1924 and 23.10.1924.
11. *op. cit.* No. 10.
12. Dr. R.S. Mani : "Educational Ideas and Ideals of Gandhi and Tagore."
13. K.C.R., p. 8.

CHAPTER 16

Dr. Maria Montessori's Philosophy of Education

Historical Sketch

Maria Montessori was born near Ancona, Italy in 1870. When she was young she was very emotional but had a very powerful intellect. At first she wanted to become an actress and joined a dramatic school. Soon she realised that her mission of life was different and she decided to take up medicine. Dr. Montessori was "the first woman on whom the degree of 'Doctor of Medicine' was conferred by the university of Rome."[1] She was an assistant in the clinic of psychiatry in that University till 1900. From 1900 to 1907 she remained a

Professor of Anthropology in the University of Rome. Both in the clinic of psychiatry and as the Professor of Anthropology she undertook a special study of feeble-minded children. "Towards the end of 1906, the Director General of the 'Roman Association of Good Building' entrusted to Montessori, the organisation of the infant schools in the model tenements in Rome.[2] In 1908, the first 'House of Children' was opened in Milan and Montessori became its President. From there onwards she renounced her medical profession. When working in this 'House of Children' she became "Deeply interested in the work of J. Itard and his pupil E. Seguin, the two Paris physicians whose researches during the first half of the nineteenth century, placed the treatment of the mentally defective upon a humane and scientific basis." With the help of her methods she herself broughtout certain didactic materials to teach the mentally defective children. In 1922, she was appointed as the 'Inspectress of Infant school'. She imparted training to teachers not only in her country but in many parts of Europe. At this time the Durham University conferred on her the degree of Doctor of Letters.

In the year 1932, when Mussoloni became the Dictator of Italy she left that place as he insisted her to educate the young for war.......... From there she moved to Spain but had to leave that country when it turned Fascist."[3] From there, she went to Holland, settled there, and founded a small school in Laren. She came to India in the year 1938 and "started her first training course in December 1939.........The experimental work and demonstrations were done in Besant Theosophical School.......In 1950 she travelled from Rome to London for a week to deliver lectures and preside over conferences."[4] She left India for good in 1951 and "It was on May 6, 1952 that she died in Holland."

She has written a number of books which include (*a*) The

Montessori Method-Vols. I & II (*b*) Reconstruction in Educacation (*c*) The child peace and Education (*d*) Education for a new world (*e*) The discovery of the child (*f*) To educate the human potential (*g*) The secret of childhood (*h*) child training (*i*) what you should know about your child and (*j*) The absorbent mind.

Educational Ideas

The educational ideas of Montessori sprang up as a revolt against the existing teaching learning practices and the treatment of problem children at schools. She dedicated her life for the upbringing of children and worked completely for their welfare. She herself says that here is a "voice that speaks for the child."[5] She criticised the then existing school practices and life of children in schools; after seeing one such school "... first of all we were shown how the school overworked and victimized the child ; she revealed him (teacher) as immolated upon the altar of labour, an unrecognized martyr, as undergoing a sort of, life sentence in a curel reformatory : the school yes, life sentence; for he suffered the servitude as long as childhood lasted."[6]

The educational ideas of Montessori are in close conformity with many of the existing psychological theories. She has been called as the liberator of the child's agony because of her 'Doctrine of Liberty'. Her emphasis on the importance of 'Auto-education' in the 'teaching-learning process' is very great. She herself prepared a number of didactic materials which helped her to vitalise her idea of 'sense training'. Though, all these ideas have been dealt with by Montessori separately, all her ideas are inter-related. Though her system has been widely criticised by many educationists, it has survived all these days because of her ideas which are widely agreed upon by psychologists.

Doctrine of Liberty

Her doctrine of liberty has risen from the theory of natural development. She feels that the child should be left free to develop according to the rhythms of nature. She believes that "We should leave as much as possible to nature; the more the babe is left free to develop, the more rapidly and perfectly will he achieve his proper propositions and higher functions."[7] What she means by according perfect liberty to the child is that "its calm and peaceful expansion should not be disturbed by the intervention of an untimely and disturbing influence."[8] She is convinced that the principle of liberty is "......rather one which by leading us from illusions to reality, will guide us to the most positive and efficacious 'care of the child.'[9] But the liberty which she advocates is " ....a well regulated liberty; the freedom which she advocates is not a freedom from physical necessities and social restraints, but a freedom which implies mastery over the environment and the self. She does not propose to 'set the children free' merely that they in turn should enslave the adult community, but rather that they may be made independent of it."[10] To her education is "the active help given to the normal expansion of the child."[11] In order to permit the free and natural manifestations of the child she has also set a limit for this freedom. The liberty that the child enjoys should ".........have as its limit, the collective interest; as its form, what we universally call good-breeding. We must, therefore, check in the child what affects or annoys others, or whatever tends towards rough or ill-bred acts. But all the rest, every manifestation having a useful scope, must not only be permitted but also be observed by the teacher."[12] The responsibility of the teacher so as to carry out the idea of 'Liberty' for the child has been well explained by Raymont in this way-"Just as the gardener's business is to provide the conditions under which the plant may develop and to leave the rest to nature, so the educator's business is to provide the conditions for the child's development, and then to refrain from interference."[13]

Auto-Education

Her idea of auto-education is closely related with that of her doctrine of liberty. When freedom is accorded and the child is left to develop according to its natural mainfestations, the child has to learn by its own experience and through the trial and error method—"for self-education the children should have the necessary freedom..........Her freedom is subject to absolute obedience to the laws of the development of the child's nature."[14] Her concept of auto education is based, according to her, on two instincts "(*a*) The effort for independence, and (*b*) the urge to work."[15] She places a lot of premium on the importance of auto-eduation in both the learning process and the structuring of personality. She says that "We must understand the child. We must recognize for what it is this vital activity. It is the constructor of personality; it forms the individual. It is a formative activity. This activity will call into play all his psychic energies they combine : he knows his aim; he wills to achieve it. He takes delight in his own effort to act independently. It is such actions as these, activities of his own independent choosing, of his own willing and purposing, which are the real, the actual constructors of the individuality of the child."[16] Montessori depends upon the environment to provide the means of self-education for the development of the individuality of the child. She wants these means to be well planned before hand instead of taking them in a random manner and says that "A science which has already provided the means of self-education should exist before-hand. ....Just as the lenses of the physicist are constructed in accordance with the law of the refraction of light so the pedagogic instrument should be based on the psychical manifestations of the child."

It may seem to us that her emphasis upon auto-education has neglected the worth of the teachers, has lessened her responsibility and has made the importance of the teacher insignificant. This notion is certainly false. She has held a high opinion of the teacher. She says that the teacher "......as the sun in the creation. She is also, for the child, a material of development. She is the spiritual material. She is the soul from which may proceed inspiration, trust and courage: she is the spirit vivifying all things........."[18] The teacher of a Montessori school is rightly called a 'Directress' because her work is consistant with her name—she should only direct the child's activity. She is more an observer of the child's activity. The work that is expected of her is "to direct, to influence and to inspire, but not, at any rate in the usual sense of the term, to instruct or teach. The object of the directress is to order the child's environment as to cause his continued absorption in his chosen occupation.[19] She wants the teacher to be trained so as to know when to intervene and when to refrain from intervening in the child's activity. In the manner of this intervention lies the personal art of the teacher.[20] The teacher's aim in a Montessori school should be "to help the child to act for himself, will for himself, think for himself; this is the art of those who aspire to serve the spirit."

Sensory Training

Montessori gives prime importance to the training of the senses of children. She herself has devised many didactic materials which serve her purpose. The purpose of these materials is "to secure a systematic and thorough training of the senses—tactile, thermic, baric, muscular, visual and audile."[22] She believes that the training of the senses should take place in isolation as far as possible. She maintains that if "we multiply the sensations and develop the capacity of appreciating fine differences in stimuli, we refine the sensibility and multiply man's pleasures."[23] Rusk has stabilised her standpoint that sensory training should replace verbal teaching in the case of infants—"The method is psychological, consequently individual;

the training must meet the child's present needs.........hence the emphasis on sensory training, the isolated activities of the practical exercises and the postponement of verbal teaching."[24] The didactic material that is provided by the Montessori system to the children will be just like play material. These play materials will be self-selected and not dictated by others; the activity that is chosen by the child will be an end in itself. Her sensory training materials are "self-corrective." Her idea of an 'Educational game' is that it is "a free activity ordered to a definite end."[25]

Her concept of discipline is entirely different from that of many of the contemporary concepts of her time. She says that "Discipline, as the first result of an order establishing itself within, is the principle phenomenon to be looked for as the 'external sign' of an internal process that has been initiated."[26] Her doctrine of liberty will not come in the way of maintaining discipline because "the liberty of the child should have as its limit the collective interest as its form, what we universally call good-breeding."[27] So the ill-bred acts of the child which might annoy other children has to be checked. But "A room in which the children move about usefully, intelligently and voluntarily, without committing any rough or rude act, commends itself to her as a well-disciplined classroom. To her noise is not at all necessarily an indication of bad discipline."[28]

She considers the child to have brought his own impressions of the world to the classroom in contrast with the realists who consider the mind of the child as a 'tabula rasa.' Her conception of the child is that "He is an observer who takes to himself in active fashion through his senses the image of outer things. An observer, mark, not a recipient as a mirror might be which passively reflects."[29]

She gives precedence to 'Writing' over 'Reading' as she

thought that reading involves the modulation of voice, accentuation of syllables and the exercise of the mechanical forms of language, both articulate and graphic; and it would be a complex task. She says that "they learn by tactual and motor experiences and grapho-motor imagery," unlike that of "learning of letters by 'visual analysis' and retained by 'visual imagery."[30]

Her Contributions to the Field of Education

She has greatly contributed to the field of education. She has been called as the liberator of the child's soul. In her times collective interest and verbal teaching stood as a bar against individual instruction. At such a time her system came to take care of the individual child—"The most characteristic feature of the method itself is its individualism,.........such individualising of instruction shares with the most recent developments in other fields of educational activity."[31] Her method is completely a result of the experiments that she has conducted on children which the experiments were completely based on experimental psychology—"The technique of our lessons is governed by experimental psychology. And this trend, without doubt, is in contrast to that of the past which was governed by speculative psychology."[32] Another significant contribution that she has made is that of her concept of a 'teacher'. The teacher of a Montessori school is not a teacher in the ordinary sense of the term but, an observer or a 'directress'. "The old time teacher who wore herself out in maintaining discipline of immobility and wasting her breath in loud and continual discourse, had disappeared and the didactic material which contains in itself the control of errors is substituted."[33] Her system will develop in the child a zeal to attend school and also an interest to learn. Thus, in a Montessori school, we may find the child working at a 'self-imposed' task for several days. Her system took far more complete charge of the child than did the ordinary school. So there will be a better scope to train the children in decent social habits.

Criticisms

While passing remarks about the Montessori system of education, one should remember what Rusk says about her system—"As the Montessori system is still in the process of evolution, it would be unwise to pass hasty criticisms on its incompleteness in certain respects."[34] But it can be criticised with the help of the existing view-points in education.

Leelavathi M. Rao remarks that "Her method is comprehensive of all the principles and doctrines put forth by the various psychologists and educators. The novelty of this method lies in its comprehensiveness."[35]

Her concept of the 'doctrine of liberty' has been appreciated by many educationists. Kilpatrick says that "......we highly approve Montessori's re-emphasis on the doctrine of liberty. In the practical outworking of her idea she has set an example to home, to Kindergarten and to primary school......."[36] He also praises her idea of auto-education. He says "It is impossible not to sympathise with Montessori's intention in emphasising this notion of auto-education. The more fully the child can learn from his own experience without any telling from the teacher, the more fully is his knowledge his own."[37]

Regarding the materials that she has devised to teach the children, they have been based upon faculty psychology which is not cojent with the existing theories. Rusk says that her "insistance on the independent values of sensory training is an example of the general tendency".

REFERENCES

1. T. Raymont : "A history of the education of young children," pp. 309-322.
2. Robert R. Rusk : "The Doctrines of Great Educators," pp. 262-289.
3. Mrs. Leelavathi M. Rao : "Montessori Method : Her life and work."
4. *Ibid.*, p. 151.
5. Dr. Maria Montessori : "Child Training" Introductory Note.
6. *Ibid.*, p. 1
7. Dr. Maria Montessori : 'Montessori Method, Vol. I, p. 4.
8. *Ibid*, p. 71.
9. *Ibid.*, p. 10.
10. Robert Rusk : "A history of infant education,, (pp. 69-88).
11. Dr. M. Montessori : Montessori Method, Vol. I, p. 104.
12. Montessori Method, Vol. I, p. 87.
13. T. Raymont : "A history of the education of young infants,,. pp. 309-322.
14. V R. Taneja : "Educational Thought and Practice", p. 153.
15. M. Montessori 'Child Training, p. 27.
16. *Ibid.*, pp. 35-36.
17. M. Montessori, Montessori Method, Vol. 1, p. 72.
18. M. Montessori : Montessori Notes, April 1934 ; quoted after T, Raymont (pp. 313-314).
19. T. Raymont, "A history of the eduction of young Children", pp. 309-322.
20. M. Montessori : Montessori Method, Vol. 1: p. 176.
21. Mrs. Leelavathi M. Rao : "Montessori Method" p. 103.
22. T. Raymont. *Ibid.*
23. R.R. Rusk : "The doctrines of Great Educatiors" pp. 262-289.
24. R.R. Rusk : "A history of infant education" pp. 69-88.

25. M. Montessori : Montessori Method, Vol. I, p. 168.
26. M. Montessori : Montessori Method, Vol. I, p. 87,
27. *Ibid.*, p. 87.
28. T. Raymont : "A history of the education of young Children" p. 316.
29. M. Montessori Child Training p. 23.
30. M. Montessori : Montessosi Method, Vol. II, pp. 296-302.
31. RR Rusk : "The Dcctrines of Great Educatiors" pp. 262-289.
32. M. Montessori : Montessori Method, Vol. I, p. 44.
33. M. Montessori : "Montessori Method" Vol. I, p. 371.
34. R.R. Rusk : "The doctrines of Great Educatiors" pp. 262-287.
35. Leelavathi M. Rao : "Montessori Method", p. 113.
36. Kilpatrick : "Montessori Examined", pp. 38-39.
37. *Ibid* pp. 48-49.

CHAPTER 17

Aurobindo's Philosophy of Education

A Life-sketch

Aurobindo was born in Calcutta in 1872. He was the son of Krishna Dhan Ghosh and Swarnalathadevi. His father had developed a fancy for the British way of life and had a contempt for everything Indian just as some of his British educated contemporaries. In fact, in one of his advertisements for the job of a cook (a bulter) in his house, he had prescribed the essential qualification as 'Knowledge of English' and not 'knowledge of cooking'. Aurobindo was thus educated at England due to his father's policy of toeing the British way of life. However, much to the dismay and chagrin of his father, and as an irony of life, Aurobindo came back to India as a revolutionary, detesting everything that was British. He became a close associate of Bipin Chandra Pal. He edited several nationalist, cultural and philosophical periodicals. 'Bande Mataram', 'Karma Yogin', 'Dharma' and 'Arya' are these periodicals. In fact, his "Essays on the Gita" first appeared as two series of articles from 1916 to 1920 in the periodical 'Arya'.

Aurobindo was arrested for treason in the famous Alipore Bomb case of 1908. Legendry Deshabandhu Chittaranjan Das, then an upcoming barrister, defended Aurobindo. Winding up his defence, CR Das frightened the sitting judge by remarking that in the case of British Government *Vs* Aurobindo, it is the British Government which is on trial and not Aurobindo. The consequences will demonstrate and posterity will judge as to who was on trial. Aurobindo was released. But the arrest proved phenomenal for Aurobindo. It led to a total metamorphosis of his inner life. Aurobindo had a vision of the absolute, a mystique experience, in the prison. After his release, he addressed a big congregation, which became famous as the Uttarapara speech. There he announced that he would no longer confine himself to fight for the political freedom of India, but work on a large canvas and towards the spiritual regeneration and freedom of India and 'man'.

Aurobindo's later life, when he had to leave Calcutta, under the British Presidency, and settle in Pondicherry, a French colony, was not punctuated by any events which can be described in a framework of time and space. It was one of philosophical development. It was the development of an inner life, a life of the mind and it is difficult to present a graphic account of that. As Aurobindo himself had put it : "My life is not on the surface of men to see".

Aurobindo was a great philosopher-sage. He was also a poet-seer. He has followed the tradition of Indian philosophers where most of them were not just academic philosophers but led a sagely life. He is also a representative of modern Indian thought. Prof. S. Chatterji has observed that : "Sri Aurobindo's life and philosophy constitute a golden link in the chain that connects the past with the present in India's cultural life".[1] According to Dr. S. Radhakrishnan and Charles A Moore[2], Aurobindo is one of the two best representatives of modern Indian thought.

Aurobindo is from the word Aravinda which is the name for the Lotus Flower in Sanskrit. Lotus grows on a swampy soil but, the mud or dirt does not stick to it. This name itself is symbolic of the way of life led by the person : attached detachment to this world – Satsang Parityag. It is to be noted that the way of life is not one of sheer detachment for allegedly advocating which Indian philosophy is often criticised. It is an ambivalent attitude to life wherein attachment to the world is simultaneously accompanied by a feeling of detachment. It is a subtle feeling, easier said than achieved. Aurobindo has glorified this state of mind in his book "Essays on the Gita" in Chapter IV : The Core of the Teaching. One is very much in the world, but still out of it.

Aurobindo's Philosophical Ideas :

Aurobindo was conscious of the diversity in Indian thought. There was exclusive emphasis on Jnana (knowledge), or Bhakthi (devotion and prayers) or Karma (work), as paths towards the divine. This exclusive emphasis deprived the individual of exposure to variety in life. It resulted in stunted, partly developed, lop-sided development of personalities. The spirit of the twentieth century Indian way of life and of philosophy has been one of synthesis. It is an attempt at integration. Dr. Radhakrishnan's philosophy is branded as Integral Humanism. Tagore christened his university as Santiniketan—an abode of peace where the East and West meet. Aurobindo also had tried to discover the integral touch in Indian philosophy. Aurobindo was interested in "seeing life steadily and see it as a whole" (Sophocles). He tried to give a 'synoptic vision of the universe' (Plato). In defending the relevence of Gita to modern life, he observes that Gita gives a synthetic understanding of universe and life. As he has put it : "Gita preserves a perfectly equal balance, emphasising now knowledge, now works, now devotion, but for the purposes of the immediate trend of the thought, not with any absolute separate preference of one over the others. He in whom all three meet and became one, He is the Supreme Being, the Purushothama".[3] In Swami Shivananda's words : "Aurobindo is the consummate expression of the Indian spirit of synthesis."[4]

Aurobindo has preached the Basic Unity of Truth. He has synthesised the conflicting points of view in Indian philosophy. The value or greatness of his philosophy lies in its comprehensiveness and emphasis on Unity of Truth. As he puts it : "First of all, there is undoubtedly a Truth one and eternal which we are seeking, from which all other Truth derives, by the light of which all other Truth finds its rightful place, explanation and relation to the scheme of knowledge".[5] Not only did he emphasise the Unity of Truth, he also glorified the need for unity of human life.[6] Aurobindo tried to integrate the varied details of the world and of life into a single whole. He tried to integrate the diverse patterns of life into a synthetic pattern. Hence, his philosophy is called as 'Purna Yoga' or 'Integral Philosophy'. 'Yoga' means a method of evolution of life. There are diverse methods of evolution of life or different yoga systems in Indian Philosophy : Hata Yoga—self-realisation through bodily or physical discipline ; Raja Yoga—through pursuit of rightful pleasures ; Karma Yoga—through work ; Bhakthi Yoga—through devotion ; and Jnana Yoga—through pursuit of knowledge. Aurobindo recognised the inherent values of each of these, tried to absorb in himself and reflect in his writings, the values of all these yogas.[7] Purna Yoga helps man to realise the Supreme, the Purushothama ; writing about it in his 'Essays on the Gita', Aurobindo concludes : "In this way you will leave in the integral truth of your own being and you will possess the integral God-Union, the whole and flawless yoga".[8] As Dr. Indra Sen has observed : "Sri Aurobindo in our times as though sensing the contemporary spirit and need undertook a wide exploration and study entitled "The Synthesis of Yoga". Here the integral personality becomes the avowed aim and the varied methods of Jnana, Bhakthi and Karma, of thought, feeling and willing, are considered and brought into a body of systematic understanding................. Here the integral man is no longer a concept, but a definite goal, a dynamic vision, a most cherished objective."[9] Integral man is a dynamic entity striving for balance in the variety of methods of self-realisation.

Aurobindo believes in evolution. In this regard, his philosophy bears the stamp of science. There is a difference between the Darwinian biological theory of evolution and Aurobindo's theory of evolution. He rejects the theory that evolution is mechanical. He goes further and believes that evolution is purposive. It is a cosmic evolution and not just a biological evolution. In believing thus he has discovered a meaning and purpose for life. As he writes in his essays on the Gita : "Life is not for the sake of life alone, but for God, ... Action is for self-finding, for self-fulfilment, for self-realisation and not only for its own external and apparent fruits of the moment or the future. There is an inner law and meaning of all things dependent on the supreme."[10] It is this inner law which guides, regulates and controls the universe and propels it into action. There is order in the universe. Kepler's laws of planetary motion, Mendeleff's law of organisation of elements, genetic laws, laws of heat, light and energy, laws of the nuclear world etc ; are illustrations of order within the microcosmic to the macrocosmic entities. The discovery of the laws which govern this universe, of the principles behind the cosmic organisation, of the moral order of the universe (even the Vedas believed in a concept called Ṛta, pronounced as Ritha, which is the moral order of the universe) etc ; is the ultimate goal of life and it lends spirituality to the person. As Aurobindo visualises : "Man will become a Superman and his mind will become a Super-mind. Super-mind will have a supermental consciousness (consciousness of Sat-Chit-Ananda : Truth, Self and Bliss ; Truth, Beauty and Goodness)."[11] Illustrations of personified mind and supermind are available in the Gita. While Arjuna, the human disciple, represents the mind— "the struggling human soul who has not received knowledge," Krishna, the divine teacher, represents the Supermind. To, Aurobindo, Mahabharatha itself is an allegory of the human life. The Superman in other words is an integral man. Dr. Indra Sen has very clearly brought out the distinctions between ordinary men and integral men in his book "The Integral Man". The Superman, the integral man is an ideal man and a society where all men are of this type is ideal society for Aurobindo visualises such an ideal man and an ideal society in his book : "The Human Cycle". In this book, analysing the growth and decay of societies Aurobindo points out that "the radical defect of all civilisations has been the neglect of the spiritual element, the soul in which is man's true being". Economic prosperity and social cohesion are important. But they are not the terminal goals of a society. Human being and his integral unfolding should be the goal of all organised efforts. A society consisting of such human beings should be the developmental goal. All the members of an integral society are integral beings.

AUROBINDO'S EDUCATIONAL IDEAS

An understanding of Aurobindo's educational ideas can be obtained from two basic sources : "On Education" and "A System of National Education". His educational system can be summed up in two words : "Integral Education". It has two functions : (*a*) It gives an integrated view of the universe to the pupil. This function of education has also been highlighted by the University Education Commission of 1948 chaired by Dr. S. Radhakrishnan. A student of science should also look at life, society and the universe around not only from a scientific perspective but also from those of humanities, fine arts and the social science. Similar perspectives are required by others also. A synthetic understanding, a holistic view of the universe and life around is required. (*b*) Education attempts at an all-round, balanced, harmonious and integrated development of the individual. Development should not be piece-meal, isolated and pigeon-holed. The physical, social, emotional, intellectual and spiritual life and powers of the child should be tapped and unfolded in an integrated way.

In brief education is a process of transforming man into an integral man. Aurobindo emphasises the need for an enormous and total transformation of man from his present state. Writing about the nature of such a transformation Aurobindo observed: "There will be needed a change of the habitual and normal nature of man as he is now to a supreme and divine spiritual nature. There will be needed in a word a yoga which shall be at once a yoga of integral knowledge, a yoga of integral will and its works, a yoga of integral love, adoration and devotion and a yoga of an integral spiritual perfection of the whole being and of all its parts and states and powers and motions."[12] Evil will go on decreasing in society and goodness, brought out by increasing numbers of integral men will be on the rise. Society will move away from slavery, untouchability, ignorance, exploitation, prejudices, vanity, jealousies and hatred and it will move towards freedom, equality, justice, brotherhood, knowledge, peace and love. All Supermen will be radiating the virtues of a Superhuman and integral society whose members are still human beings in physical form.

Though Aurobindo was a great nationalist and a champion of Indian culture, he did not blindly glorify it. He was not a blind lover of Indian culture. He was aware of its defects and the need for its reformation, rejuvenation and renaissance. One of his books is titled as "Renaissance in India". His love of Indian culture was par excellence. He was distressed at the blind criticisms of Indian culture by the Westerners. Macaulay, McKenzie, Schweitzer, Archer and many more westerners like them had criticised Indian Culture in several ways such as life-negating, worthless and far inferior in content and quality to western culture. Aurobindo wrote a 'rationalistic critic on Indian Culture' in reply to William Archer, in the form of a book titled : "Foundations of Indian Culture". The title of the third chapter of this book is : "A Defence of Indian Culture". Even in his writings on education he observed : "They should be children of the past, possessors of the present, creators of the future. The past is our foundation, the present our material, the future our aim and summit."[13]

Aims of Education

Right down the ages one aim of education has been overriding the minds of Indian saints and philosophers. This has been rightly identified by Prof. Humayun Kabir in his book "Indian Philosophy of Education" as 'self-realisation'. This discovery is applicable in a trite manner in case of Aurobindo also. In one of his writings he has highlighted the aim of education thus : "Education will at no time lose sight of man's highest object, the awakening and development of his spiritual being,"[14] At another place he has observed : "The chief aim of education should be to help the growing soul to draw out that in itself which is best and make it perfect for a noble use".[15]

What does Aurobindo mean by Education as Self-realisation ?

His concept of self-realisation is based on the teaching of the Upanisads. The Taittiriya Upanised has described the self as surrounded by five layers (constituted of five sheaths), the panchakosas. Aurobindo believed in the validity of this Upanisadic teaching and when he speaks of an education of the self, he means an education relating to all these five layers when alone he says education becomes an *integral education.* The schemata is as follows :

Cells/layers	*English translation*	*Appropriate education*
Annamaya Kosha	Physical Cell	Physical education
Pranamaya Kosha	Vitality Cell	Vital education (of sense organs)
Manamaya Kosha	Mental Cell	Intellectual education
Vijnanamaya Kosha	Psychic Cell	Social and Emotional Education
Anandamaya Kosha	Spiritual Cell	Spiritual education.

Education is a progressive, inter-related, coordinated and meaningful stimulation and growth of all these cells. Together, they lead to integral education. As Aurobindo writes : "Education to be complete must have principal aspects relating to the five primary activities of the human being : the physical, the vital, the mental, the psychic and the spiritual. Usually these phases of education succeed each other in a chronological order following the growth of the individual. This however, does not mean that one should replace another but that all must continue, completing each other, till the end of life."[16]

Methods of Education

A special feature of Aurobindo's system of education is that it is highly psychological. His methods of education in particular are rooted in individual attention, promote creativity, encourage dialogues, attempt at alround development of the individual. Aurobindo advocated the method of discovery and activity. He believed in self-teaching : show how to learn, do not impart knowledge. As he put it : "Teacher should put the child into the right road to his own perfection and encourage him to follow it, watching, suggesting, helping, but not interfering."[17]

Aurobindo International Centre of Education, at Pondicherry, popularly known as Aurobindo Ashram, was the place where during his life-time and then during that of the Mother (a French woman who took fancy for Aurobindo's teachings in his initial years, became his ardent disciple, left France and settled in India at Pondicherry, gave away all her wealth, time and energies for the promotion of the noble purposes which Aurobindo championed and lived for) Aurobindo's educational and life-related ideas were being translated in real life.

REFERENCES

1. S. Chatterji : "The Integral Philosophy of Sri Aurobindo" a Commemmorative Symposium edited by Haridas Chaudhuri (same title), Allen & Unwin, London, 1969.
2. S. Radhakrishnan and C.A. Moore : "A Source-book in Indian Philosophy". Refer to a special chapter on Aurobindo's Philosophy.
3. Aurobindo : "Essays on the Gita" Chapter 4.
4. See reference No. 1 here, Chapter 25.
5. See reference No. 3 here, Chapter 1.
6. Aurobindo : "The Ideal of Human Unity"
7. Aurobindo : "The Synthesis of Yoga"
8. See reference No. 3 here, Chapter 24 "The Message of the Gita" p. 558.
9. Indra Sen : "The Integral Man", pp. 24-25.
10. See reference No. 3 here, Chapter 24.
11. Aurobindo : "The Future Evolution of Man". Also See, "The Human Cycle" by Aurobindo.
12. See reference No. 3 here, p. 557.
13. Aurobindo : "On Education", p. 12.
14. Aurobindo : "A Preface on National Education" in "*ARYA*" 1920-21.
15. Aurobindo : "A syetem of National Education", p. 11.
16. See reference No. 13 here, pp. 55-56.
17. See reference No. 15 here, p. 17.

CHAPTER 18

Paulo Freire

Abysmal poverty, shameless exploitation and immiserisation of masses of humanity by a small, but historically well and advantageously placed minority, illhealth, diseases, ignorance and illiteracy among masses, large-sized families, high fertility and low infant survival rates, malnutrition, under-nutrition and low life-expectancy, underemployment, low wages, inegalitarian structures of land, income and property positions, social stratification and segregation of poor and disadvantaged, flourishing and prosperous small areas amidst large regions of backwardness, highly diffuse social groups lacking identity-consciousness, submerged in irrational traditions, superstitions and fear of establishment, social and political oppression..............., are all the characteristic features of developing, subsistence, till recently colonised societies where people eke out an 'existence' in the hope of a better tomorrow, rather than 'live' a life of meaning, purpose and direction.

National and International communities committed to a life of humanism, equality, liberty, fraternity, social, economic and political justice are struggling with the mighty force of history to redress the poor of the developing regions and rejuvenate life in them. Several strategies are tried and tested in this regard. Poverty alleviation and economic freedom through economic protection, subsidies and incentives, employment, wage-policies, assets redistribution and supply, etc. ; are some of the measures herein. They have proved to be inadequate and partially successful. In a complementary strategy it is suggested that the real solution for the ills of contemporary societies lies in unfolding and elevating the spirit, will-power, consciousness, environmental awareness and appropriate attitudes to set right the environment. In brief, what is required is 'empowerment' of the people through education, conscientisation and political mobilisation.

It is the second non-economic strategy which was advocated, tried, tested and perfected by Paulo Freire. He was bord at Recife, Brazil in 1921. He was jailed immediately after the military coup in 1964 and released seventy days later and encouraged to leave the country. He returned to Brazil after political stability was restored. He inspired generations of poverty-stricken Brazilians towards nobler and higher levels of life and society. He summarized his philosophy, methods of work and the abstract realities of his working environment in a celebrated and widely acclaimed book titled "Pedagogy of the oppressed." The Penguin edition was published in 1972. The novelty or distinctiveness of his approach lies in his methods of change wherein the oppressed majority bring about a change in their political, social and economic environment without resorting to violence and through winning the hearts of the oppressors with love, education and peaceful methods. Methods of discussion, negotiation, persuasion, and conviction are resorted to by the people. Those who attempt to redress the ills of the suffering humanity are not leaders who work for the people, but act as servants who work with the people. This is Paulo Freire's philosophy which he prefers to title as 'Scientific Revolutionary Humanism'. This is essentially a philosophy involving techniques of adult and non-formal education though the ingrained messages bear utility-potential for any form of education.

Oppressor's Framework

Freire has tried to capture the psychology, dynamics of operations, methods of work, framework of thinking of the 'oppressors' of society. They are the people who represent, regulate and manage the establishment. Freire identifies four ways in which the oppressors operate : conquest, divide and rule, manipulation and cultural invasion. They are not interested in entering into dialogues and discussions with the people. Their actions are anti-dialogical. They spread myths such as 'high caste people are normally the intelligent sections of society.' They may not complete their sentence which is implied herein : 'hence, they are fit to occupy privileged and decision-making positions in society and rule others.' If they don't succeed, or even otherwise, they resort to repressive action and demonstrate their ability to put down any form of rebellious movemeat. At times they may also bestow upon the oppressed, gifts, incentives, gratifications, benefits etc ; and exhibit paternalism. In other words they employ populist measures to appease the masses and win their confidence. All these actions are intended to conquer the people, either through force or hoarse. This is termed by Freire as the technique of 'Conquest'. Another technique used by the oppressors is to divide the people and rule them. Problems are viewed in focalised rather than a holistic way. Caste, class, language, religion, race, ethnicity or any other such differences are employed to divide the people. Their attention is thus diverted from problems that commonly affect them. If in spite of these two measures, people get organised and begin to protest against the establishment and try to change it, then a third technique is used : manipulation. The environment is so manipulated that any semblence of a rebellion is shifted and strangulated. Pacts, accords, aggrements, settlements, etc ; are made in such ways that would temporarily pacify the agitators and facilitate the rulers to continue in power. Yet another technique that is used to oppress people is termed as cultural invasion. The purpose is to metamorphose and transform the people in such ways as to make them think that the rulers, their ways of thinking and life are the models for change. This is done in the name of modernisation and social change. It implies an utter and total disregard for folk-ways, folk-art, folk-music, folk-language and in brief, folk-culture.

Freire's Framework

Freire has presented an alternative framework of thinking and action which he terms as the theory of dialogical cultural action. It implies four-fold measures : Cooperation, unity for liberation, organisation and cultural synthesis.

Those who would like to work with the people should first enlist their co-operation. This is possible through meaningful communication with them wherein the leaders are normally listeners in the process. The leaders should identify themselves with the life-patterns of the people and share a concern for their needs, hopes and aspirations. They should strike a communion with the people. Secondly, it is essential to promote solidarity among the people by emphasising the class to which all of them belong. They should become conscious of common needs and interests such as those of health, education, housing, employment and rightful wages, child and old care, and all other common property resources on which they have a rightful share. This consciousness should unite them and transcend them over the petty, narrow and superficial differences. Thirdly, it is required to organise the people. They should be mobilised and unionised so that they can speak with one voice. This is to be done through instilling confidence in the people. The record of work of the leaders and their demonstrated sincerity can build up faith among the people. People can be won through pristine love. Leaders should shed the consciousness of their qualifications, parentage, connections, qualifications, class-affiliation, achievement, and be friendly and informal in their approach. Finally, it is required to blend a cultural synthesis between the people's world and the leaders' world. Such a synthesis ought to emerge without any impositions from above and rather through an honest appreciation and accommodation of people's world-view.

Methods of Change

A variety of multi-sensory-stimulation techniques such as graphic and audio-visual aids including charts, diagrams, maps, pictures, slides, etc. are advocated to educate the people and conscientise them But the focus of conscientisation should be the surrounding world. The substance or content should be defined by the people. This is possible if the leaders employ the dialogical method. Dialogue with the people is the first step in education. 'Dialogue is an encounter among men who name the world.' People should describe the world and reality around them, create values rather than receive them, and thus develop their understandings and commitments for action. Their understandings need only to be reorganised, interpreted, discussed and refined. Freire quotes Mao to press this point :

"We must teach the masses clearly what we have received from them confusedly". People have a better understanding of the reality around them which nurture the seeds of oppression. They are not able to organise their perceptions, articulate them clearly, plan corrective action, execute and sustain it. As such the starting point for organising programme content, should be the 'present, existential, concrete situation'. The impact of existentialism is clearly visible in Freire's thinking. In fact, he quotes Sartre's distinction between the banking concept of education and the digestive and nutritive concept. In the banking process of education knowledge is deposited in the recipients, mind just as money is deposited in Banks. But in the digestive or nutritive process, knowledge, skills and understandings or so deposited as would suit the digestive system of the recipients, function as nutrients for growth and development. This is done through involving the native abilities and raising the critical consciousness of the people.

Planning for Teaching

Freire suggests a ten-stage cyclical process assisted by an interdisciplinary team of specialists in human problems to develop and deliver the thematic content. It involves the codification and decodification (TAT type) of people's understandings of reality in which they live. The teams work among groups called as culture circles.

Conclusions

Freire is relevant to the teachers and educators in developing countries. This is especially true in case of adult, non-formal and extension education programmes, though the values of his techniques and philosophy cannot be ruled out for younger age-groups. He betrays no ill-will, malice, hatred or violence against the oppressors while showing his concern, commitment and constructive action for the oppressed. Rather he advocates that the hearts of oppressors should be won through love, non-violence and peaceful resistance and radical action. In doing so, Freire appears to be too close to Gandhiji's views on life as well as on social, economic and political change. In fact, recently a comparative analysis has been made of Gandhi and Freire in regard to their philosophy, techniques and contexts of work (Mathew Zacharaiah : "Revolution through Reform", A comparison of Sarvodaya and Conscientisation. Sage Publications, New Delhi, 1988). In fact Prof Zachariah places Gandhi higher than Freire as the former emphasised the transformation of the human being and society as a totality and in an integral way, wherein not just changes in the material world which Freire had emphasised but along with changes in material world, other kinds of changes in the intellectual, social, moral and spiritual domains of life were contemplated. Even the dialogical techniques advocated by Freire is not new to India. This was the technique during the Upanisadic period and under the Gurukula system of education. Changes observed are mostly in regard to contents of teaching and in the use of audio-visual and semi-projective techniques.

However, good things deserve appreciation and following whether they are repetitive in nature or across regional and national boundaries. This is true of Freire's philosophy, life and work also.

CHAPTER 19

Sarvepalli Radhakrishnan

India rediscovered herself in the latter half of the nineteenth and early period of the twentieth century. This was a period of renaissance, enlightenment, identity—consciousness, image-building and synthesis. Scores of scholars, saints, savants, statesmen, artists, historians, literatteurs, scientists, philosophers and others participated and contributed to the process of rediscovery. Rediscovery implied a two-fold approach. On the one hand it implied an awareness and understanding of the spirit of the times : the values and practices relevant to modern, industrial, inter-dependent world, highlighting therein democracy and individual liberty, socialism referring to equality and justice, secularism and national unity. On the other hand it implied an awareness and critical understanding of the richness.

variety and timelessness of the cultural heritage of India that would strengthen the spirit of modern times. Breadth of vision and depth of understanding were required of the person to match this task. Radhakrishanan was one such person who could successfully see through time and space in the context of India and across the contemporary world. In this way, he reinterpreted Indian philosophy and culture in authoritative and convincing ways that appealed to the modern man. He rejuvenated the native, traditional wisdom of the land through a process of critical appraisal, screening, filtering and purification. He could capture the synthetic, integral, holistic, time-tested, synoptic vision that has invaded Indian intellectual thinking over the centuries. Thus, he rose to heights of excellance in Indian national life as well as in international spheres. Hence, a tribute in his centenary year is fair and befitting.

Life. Radhakrishnan was born at Tiruthani near Madras on September 5, 1888, in an orthodox but educated Brahmin family. This day is celebrated as TEACHERS' DAY in India as he rose to eminence and acted as the President of India with humble beginnings as a college and university teacher and running through an academic career spanning over four decades.

Radhakrishnan was educated at Madras. He taught philosophy at the universities in Madras, Mysore, Calcutta and Benaras. He held lectureship at Universities of Oxford and Chicago. He was appointed Spalding Professor of Eastern Religions and Ethics at Oxford in 1936. He was also a Fellow of the All Souls College then. He served as Ambassador to Moscow and Vice-President of India before he was elected to the Office of the President in 1962. His five-year term of office as second President of the country was marked by turbulence, economic crisis and changing power-relations. There was an on-going border conflict with China, food-crisis. a war with

Pakistan, followed by deaths in succession of two Prime Ministers of the country—Jawaharlal Nehru in 1964 and Lal Bahadur Shastri in 1966. Indira Gandhi assumed office as Prime Minister during his Presidency. He was knighted in 1931 and awarded Bharath Ratna, the highest national award posthumously, after his death at Madras on April 17, 1975. He was also the first non-christian to receive the Templeton Prize for Religion.

Works

Radhakrishnan was a prolific writer. Between 1923 and 1927 he wrote his famous two volumes of 'Indian Philosophy' which ran into several editions and reprints and even to this day are among the standard texts on the subject. He wrote "The Philosophy of the Upanisads" in 1924. Two of his popular books are—'The Hindu View of Life' and 'The Idealist View of Life' published in 1929. 'Freedom and Culture' was published in 1936. His book on 'Eastern Religions and Western Thought, came out in 1939. Through this book he came to be established in the Western world with his comparative perspectives. This particular book is a landmark in his life and achievements. Right through the 19th and early period of twentieth centuries some of the Western thinkers who did not belong to the tribe of Max Muellar, Monier Williams, A.L. Basham, Hopkins, Sir John Marshall, Mortimer Wheeler, etc., were very critical of Indian way of life and thinking to the extent of being prejudiced against it. W.S. MckenZie, Lord Macaulay, William Archer, Albert Schweitzer were some illustrative and eminent Western writers and opinion-builders. For instance, Albert Schweitzer wrote in his book 'Development of Indian Thought' that Indian ways of thinking and its religions affirm and advocate life-negation. India preaches escapism and encourages one to run away from the day-to-day, real problems of life. It does not prepare one to face the challenges of life but instead takes him away to a life of recluse and isolation. Several selected illustrations from the variety of Indian writings and life-stories were presented as evidence to support this theory. This was the message put across the Western world regarding India by many Western writers. Radhakrishnan desired to put an end to this distorted, dangerous and propagandist view of India, however unintentional it may be. Hence he chose to write a befitting reply to one of these series of writings. He chose Schweitzer's 'Development of Indian Thought' for this purpose, to start with. In his reply, which assumed, the form of 'Eastern Religions and Western Thought' he has identified perfectly similar or identical illustrations of thinking and life-patterns in the variety of Western writing and life-stories that Schweitzer had quoted from the Indian scene to justify his assessments. Thus, he demolished the theory that India preached 'life-negation'. Further, he went on to demonstrate and elaborate how India stood for life-affirmation, love, compassion, concern for the poor and down-trodden and above all tolerance and synthesis. The little extra emphasis that India has placed on spiritualism and idealistic way of life should not be misread as anti-materialistic or anti-humanistic. Radhakrishnan showed how Indian thinking down the ages has reiterated the essential oneness of humanity and thereby upheld the values of liberty, equality, fraternity and justice. He followed this book much later with a work on the areas of synthesis between 'East and West : Some Reflections', in 1956.

By 1946, he had made a survey of the thinking of eminent and distinguished Indians including Mahatma Gandhi regarding their world-view, views on life and society and their message for the rest. He weaved them into a network and brought out his book 'Contemporary Indian Philosophy' in 1950. Another contribution of Radhakrishnan which is of great value for anyone who does not know Sanskrit or Pali but is interested in reading original texts of Indian Philosophy, is the English version he edited along with Charles Moore : 'A Source Book in Indian Philosophy.' It is a rare treasure which contains English translations of significant extracts from the Vedas, the Upanisads, the systems of Indian Philosophy including therein the three hetorodox and the six orthodox systems and with a special attention to the Vedantic schools, the Epics, as well as selections from Radhakrishnan and Aurobindo representing contemporary thought. The appendix of this book also includes a note on pronunciation and accent in regard to Sanskrit words, a list of 56 original sources of manuscripts for which English translations are made, a long list of 36 original books from which selections are made for compiling this book. A comprehensive bibliography at the end on the variety of Indian Philosophy is a boon to the researcher on the subject. His last book was published in 1967 : 'Religion in a Changing World'. He has also published scores of articles on variety of issues and problems of Indian Philosophy. Radhakrishnan is universally acknowledged for his gripping and poetic command over the English language. He mastered the art of impressive and lucid communication at a very early age. To provide an illustrative piece from one of his articles published in the 'International Journal of Ethics' in 1914 : "If instead of reason, our senses guide us, our life will be a mirror of passing passions and temporary inclinations. He who leads such a life has to be written down, like Dogberry, an ass. His life will be a series of disconnected and scattered episodes, will have no purpose to take, no work to carry out, no end to realise. In a rational life, every course of action before it is adopted, is brought before the bar of reason, and its capacity to serve the highest end is tested and, if found suitable, adopted by individuals". His convocation addresses at various Indian Universities cover a wide range of problems of Indian Education. They have been published along with other writings in two volumes as 'Occasional speeches and writings'. He also served as Chairman of the University Education Commission which submitted its report in 1948.

Radhakrishnan's World-View

The chief contribution of the philosopher—statesman is his originality in the interpretation of the traditional Indian world-view which had suffered several distortions. In his commentaries on the Brahma Sutras, Sankara had viewed the surrounding world and experiences therein as '*Maya*'. There is no equivalent term for this word in English or other European languages. This is because there is no equivalent concept in the Western world-view at all. As such this term has been translated as 'illusion', therein divesting the world around of all its realistic basis and distoring Sankara's world-view to match it with the views of Western philosophers down the ages right from Plato through Descartes, Bergson, Bosanquet, Bradley, Kant, Schophenhauer and Hegel who had conceived of the external world as a manifestation of a Great Idea, alone being real while the manifesting medium, one of essential unreality. Radhakrishnan asserted and emphatically so that Indian philosophers including Sankara have not equated Maya with unreality. Instead, Maya is equated with the relative meaninglessness of the external and empirical universe in the overall ontological design of the cosmos. The meaning of the external world is subordinate to the level of mental outlook of a person. For instance, for a child, in the mental universe in which it exists, the glossy, silken outer cover of a chocolate has meaning and it derives pleasure in collecting, storing, exchanging and discussing about it. The same activity is purposeless and meaningless in the adult-world. For the full grown mundane adult the chocolate cover is replaced by money, land, wealth, gold, wine, women, entertainment, rich food and a variety of other symbols of pleasure. But for a person who has transcended these levels of sensory stimulation and pleasure they are purposeless and meaningless. Just as the adult looks at the chocolate cover as only essential to protect the inner stuff from dust and decay, the transcended human will look at the worldly objects as just essential elements for existence. He has no more meaning for them. They do not excite him. It does not mean that they are unreal. It is a position of relativity in meanings. Thus arguing, Radhakrishnan regenerated the Indian view of the world and life in it from criticism of life-negation, escapism, etc. We live in a dynamic, vibrant, charged, vigorous and perceptible world beyond which there is a tranquil, equanimous, meaningful, imperceptible and abstract universe that will reveal itself to the inner eye, the vision or intuition. Science is necessary to understand, adjust and live in harmony with the surrounding universe. But it is not sufficient to reach the Absolute which is both the universe and the transcendent, self-propelled and self-regulating principle underneath it. You require science, as well as meta-science to realise the Absolute. This is a very subtle and needle-hole distinction required to understand the universe and the life within it. In essence, the same message is conveyed in the sense of detached attachment or Satsanga Parityaga advocated by the Gita One has to be attached to the world, and at the same time detached from it. It is like Aravinda, the Lotus, which blossoms out of the swampy soil without the pasty mud sticking into it.

Radhakrishnan's School of Thought

Among the well recognised schools of thought, Radhakrishnan's philosophy is classified under Idealism. Though Idealism advocates ideals in life, the etimology of the phrase has nothing to do with ideals. It is from the assertion that ideas are real, the ultimate reality is a great and grand idea, the humans being an expression of this great idea. All human beings, irrespective of their race, religion, class, caste, language, nationality, sex, ethnicity, etc., are sparks of the divine. Hence service to humanity is service to God. In fact, by self-realisation, which is the goal of almost all the scholars of Indian philosophy, Radhakrishnan means the 'social self'. As he wrote : "Moral conduct is self-realised conduct if by the self we mean not the empirical self, with all its weaknesses and vulgarity, selfishness and smallness, but the deeper nature of man, free from all fetters of selfish individuality." (Indian Philosophy, Vol. 1, 1940, p. 210). This is his philosophy and message wherein he looked at the sea of humanity in an integral and holistic perspective. His philosophy has been termed as 'Integral Humanism'.

His view of Education

Right through the ages, India has been seized with a spirit of synthesis, harmony, integration and holism in its view of life and universe. This is reflected in the values it has all along glorified such as humanism, tolerance, non-violence, compassion and love. It is a view wherein one looks at the other person not as a neighbour, a friend or a brother but as oneself. Such realisation is the summit of a conical hierarchy of learnings, understandings, exercises, reflections, contemplation and flashes that are built up brick by brick from the earliest level of education through its final stages. Knowledge of sciences and the social sciences, humanities and the arts, philosophy and religion are all required in their balancing proportions to realise a wholesome and meaningful education. Thus, Radhakrishnan had declared that the 'purpose of education is to give an integral view of the universe', in the opening pages of the Report of University Education Commission.

In brief, Radhakrishnan was one of the distinguished sons of India who discovered the golden links between the hoary and glorious past of this country with the scientific, technological, democratic, secular, socialistic and modern outlook of man.

Bibliography

1 ADAMS, SIR JOHN : *Modern Developments in Educational Practice.* University of London Press, London, 1928.

2. ALBERTY, HAROLD : *Reorganizing the High school Curriculum*, Macmillan Co., New York, 1953.

3. ALLEN, E.A. : *Existentialism From Within*, R and K Paul, London, 1953.

4. ALLPORT : *Personality, Pattern and Growth*, Holt Rinehart and Winston, New York, 1963.

5. ARISTOTLE : *Politics* (ed.) Earnest Barker, Oxford University Press, Oxford, 1948.

6. AUROBINDO : *Essays on the Gita*, Sri Aurobindo Ashram, Pondicherry, 1970.

7. AYER, A.J. : *Language, Truth and Logic.* Gollancz, London, (II ed.), 1946.

8. AYER, A.J. : *Philosphical Essays*, Macmillan and Co. Ltd., London, 1959.

9. BLACKHAM, H.J. : *Six Existentialist Thinkers*, Macmillan & Co., London, 1951.

10. BLAU, JOSEPH L. : *Men and Movements in American Philosophy*, Prentice Hall, Inc., New York, 1963.

11. BOGOSLOVSKY : *The Ideal School*, Macmillam Co., New York, 1936.

12. BROUDY : *Building a Philosophy of Education*, Prentice Hall, New Delhi, 1965.

13. BRUBACHER, J.S. : *Modern Philosophies of Education*, Mc Graw Hill, New Delhi, 1969.

14. BRUBACHER, J.S. : 'Education for Death' *School and Society*, LVI, Aug. 22, 1942, pp. 137-141.

15. BUTLER, DONALD : *Four Philosophies and their Practice in Education and Religion*, Harper and Row, New York, 1968.

16. CHILDS, J.L. : *Education and the Philosophy of Experimentalism.* Appleton Century, New York, 1931.

17. O' CONNOR, D.J. : *An Introduction to the Philosophy of Education*, Routledge and Kegan Paul London, 1966.

18. DEWEY, JOHN : *Democracy and Education*, The Macmillan Co., New York, 1944.

19. DEWEY, JOHN : *Child and the Curriculum*, Phenix Books, University of Chicago Press, Chicago, 1956.

20. DEWEY, JOHN : *School and Society*, Phenix Books, University of Chicago Press, Chicago, 1956.

21. DEWEY, JOHN : *Problems of Men*, Philosophical Library, New York, 1946.

22. DEWEY, JOHN : *Creative Intelligence*, Holt. Rinehart, Winston, New York, 1917.

23. DICKENS, CHARLES : *Hard times.*

24. FROEBEL : *A Selection from his Writings* by Irene M Lilly, Cambridge University Press, Cambridge, 1967.

25. GITA : Gorakhpur Press.

26. GRENE, MARJORIE : *Dreadful freedom. A critique of existentialism*, University of Chicago Press, Chicago, 1948.

27. GURUDUTT, K. : *Existentialism and Indian Thought* Philosophical Library, New York, 1960.

28. GWYNN, J. MINOR : *Curriculum Principles and Social Trends*, Macmillan, New York, 1948.

29. HANS, NICHOLAS : *Comparative Education*, R and K Paul, London, 1958, (III ed.).

30. HARPER, RALPH : 'Existence and Recognition, in *NSSE 54th Year Book*, Public School Pub. Co., Bloomington III.

31. HEIDEGGER : *Existence and Being.* Vision Press, London, 1949.

32. HENDERSON, S.V.P. : *Introduction to the Philosophy of Education*, University of Chicago Press, Chicago 1947.

33. HIRIYANNA, M. : *Outlines of Indian Philosophy*, Allen and Unwin, London, 1932.

34. HIRIYANNA, M. : 'The Aim of Indian Philosophy' in *Popular essays in Indian Philosophy*, Kavyalaya Publishers, Mysore, 1952.

PH HIRST & RS PETERS : "*The Logic of Education*" ELBS and R & K Paul, London, 1975.

PH HIRST : "Knowledge and the Curriculum" R & K Paul, London, 1974.

35. HOCKING, W.E. : *Types of Philosophy*, Charles Scribners and Sons, New York, 1937.

36. HORNE, H.H. : *The New Education*, Abingdon Press, New York, 1931.

37. HORNE, H.H. : *The Philosophy of Education*, Macmillan and Co., New York, 1937.

38. HUSSAIN, S. ABID : *The National Culture of India*, Jaico, Bombay, 1956.

39. JAMES, WILLIAM : *Pragmatism*, Longmans Greens & Co., New York, 1914.

40. KILPATRICK : *Philosophy of Education*, Macmillan and Co., New York, 1963.

41. KNELLER : *Existentialism and Education*, Philosophical Library, New York, 1958.

42. KNELLER (ed.) : 'Contemporary Educational Theory' in *Foundations of Education*. John Wiley and Sons, New York, 1967.

43. KING and BROWNELL : *The curriculum and the Disciplines of Knowledge*. John Wiley and Sons, New York, 1966.

44. LONGFORD, Glenn and O'connor, D.J. (ed.): *New essays in the Philosophy of Education*, Routledge and Kegan Paul, London, 1973.

45. MILL, J.S. : *On Education*. Cavenagh, E.A. ed, Greenwood, 1931.

46. MONROE : *A Text Book in the History of Education* (educational series), Norwood Edns., 1905.

47. MONTESSORI : *Montessori Method.* Vols. I & II, William Heinemann, London, 1918.

48. MUNSHI, K.M. : *Foundations of Indian Culture,* Bhavan's Publications.

49. NEA : *Learning the Ways of Democracy,* Educational Policies Commission, USA, 1940.

50. NSSE : *42nd Year Book.* Part I, Public School Pub. Co., Bloomington III, 1942.

51. NEHRU JAWAHAR LAL . *Discovery of India,* Meridian Books, London, 1956.

52. NIBLETT, W.R. : 'On Existentialism and Education in *British Journal of Education Studies.* Vol. II, No. 2 May 1954.

53. NUNN, T.P. : *Education, its Data and First Principles.* The Modern Educators Library Series, Edward Arnold and Co., London, 1920.

54. PANIKKAR, K.M. : *Essential Features of Indian Culture,* Bhavan's Publication.

55. PARK, JOE : *Selected Readings in the Philosophy of Education,* Macmillan and Co., New York, 1968.

56. PATRICK, G.T.W. : *Introduction to Philosophy,* Allen and Unwin, London, 1951.

57. PETERS, R.S. : 'Must an educator have an Aim ?' in *Authority, Responsibility and Education.* Allen and Unwin, London, 1959.

58. PHENIX : *Philosophy of Education,* Holt and Rinehart, New York, 1958.

59. PLATO : Republic (tr.) B Jowett, in 'The Dialogues of Plato' Vol. II, Clarendon Press (IV ed.) Oxford, 1953.

60. PRATTE, RICHARD : *Contemporary Theories of Education.* IEP, London, 1971.

61. RAJENDER PRASAD, Dr : *India Divided,* Hind Kitabs Ltd., Bombay, 1947.

62. REID, LEWIS, ARNOLD : *Philosophy and Education.* Heinemann, London, 1961.

63. REID, L.A. : *Philosophy and the Theory and Practice of Education.* Evan Brothers Ltd., London, 1965.

64. Report of the Secondary Education Commission, 1952.

65. Report of the Kothari Commission, 1966.

66. Report of the University Education Commission, 1948.

67. RORTY, RICHARD ed : *The Linguistic Turn*, University of Chicago Press, Chicago, 1970.

68. ROSS : *Ground Work of Educational Theory*, George G. Harrap and Co. Ltd., London, 1958.

69. ROUSSEAU, J.J. : *Emile* (tr.) Barbara Foxley Everyman's Library, Dent, London, 1911.

70. ROUSSEAU, J.J. : *Social Contract*, Allen and Unwin, London, 1959.

71. RUGGEIRO : *Existentialism* (ed.) Happen Stall, Seeker and Warburg, London, 1946.

72. RUNES : *Pictorial History of Philosophy*, Philosophical Library, New York, 1959.

73. RUSSELL, BERTNAND : *Why I am not a Christian ?*

74. RUSSELL, BERTRAND : *History of Western Philosophy*, Unwin University Books, Allen and Unwin, London, 1969.

75. SARTRE : *Existentialism and Humanism*, (tr.) Philip Mariet, Metheun & Co., London, 1948.

76. SARTRE, JEAN PAUL : *Existentialism.* The Philosophical Library, New York, 1952.

77. SARTRE, JEAN PAUL : *Being and Nothingness.* (ed.) Dr. H.E. Barnes Philosophical Library, New York, 1956.

78. SARTRE, JEAN PAUL : *Of Human Freedom*, (tr.) W. Baskin Philosophical Library, New York, 1966.

79. SARTRE, JEAN PAUL : *Condemned to Freedom* (ed.), Justus Streller Philosophical Library, New York, 1960.

80. SAYRE, KENNETH, M. : *Plato's Analytic Method*, University of Chicago Press, Chicago, 1969.

81. SCHEFFLER, ISRAEL : *The Language of Education*, Charles C. Thomas, Illinois, 1960.

82. SINGH, R.P. : *Democratic Philosophy of Education*, Kitab Mahal, Allahabad, 1966.

83. SMITH, VINCENT : *Oxford History of India*, Oxford University Press, London, 1906.

84. SMITH, Othanel and ENNIS, Robert, H. (eds.) : *Language and Concepts in Education*, Rand Mc Nally & Co., Chicago, 1961.

85. SMITH, P.G. : *Philosophy of Education*, Harper and Row, New York, 1965.

86. SPENCER, HERBERT : *On Education* (ed.) Andreas M. Kazamies, Classics in education, Series No. 30, Teachers College Press, Columbia University, New York, 1966.

87. SRINIVASAN, G. : *Existentialist Concepts and the Hindu Philosophical Systems*, Udayana Publications, Allahabad, 1967.

88. THIRTHA, N.V. : *National Integration*, Jullundur University, 1954.

89. TOYNBEE, ARNOLD : *A Study of History*, Oxford University Press, 1946.

90. TYLOR, E.B. : *Primitive Cultures*, Vol. I, Harper and Bros., New York, 1958.

91. WAHL, JEAN : *A Short History of Existentialism*, Philosophical Library, New York, 1949.

92. WITTGENSTEIN, L. : *Tractatus Logico Philosophicus*, Kegan Paul, Trench, Trubrer & Co., London, 1922.

Index

E

F

G

H